ART SPARKS

DRAW, PAINT, MAKE, AND GET CREATIVE WITH 53 AMAZING PROJECTS!

Marion Abrams & Hilary Emerson Lay

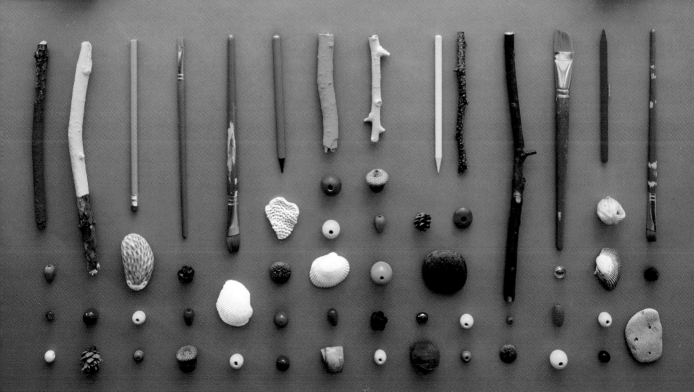

The mission of Storey Publishing is to serve our customers by publishing practical information that encourages personal independence in harmony with the environment.

EDITED BY Deanna F. Cook and Michal Lumsden
ART DIRECTION AND BOOK DESIGN BY Michaela Jebb
TEXT PRODUCTION BY Erin Dawson and Ian O'Neill

COVER PHOTOGRAPHY BY © Andrew Greto Photography (spine), Ian O'Neill (front), and Mars Vilaubi (back)
COVER AND CHAPTER OPENER LETTERS CREATED BY Kimberly Stoney
INTERIOR PHOTOGRAPHY BY © Andrew Greto Photography

ADDITIONAL PHOTOGRAPHY BY © Album/Alamy Stock Photo, 68; Art Institute of Chicago/Wikimedia Commons, 20 (insets); © Chiyacat/ Dreamstime.com, 88 top; © Danny Lehman/Corbis/VCG/Getty Images, 26 top left; © David Talukdar/Getty Images, 94 right; © Fine Art/Contributor/ Getty Images, 39 bottom; Ian O'Neill, 1; © littlemsshutterbug/iStock.com, 156 left; Mars Vilaubi, 3 bottom right, 56, 59, 66 top right; Michaela Jebb, 10, 11, 13, 31, 47, 49 bottom right, 73, 103, 133, 135 (clothespins and pipe cleaners); © mybaitshop/stock.adobe.com, 8 (toothpicks); © Povareshka/iStock.com, 104 bottom left (flowers); © studio BM/Shutterstock.com, 166; © Universal History Archive/UIG/Bridgeman Images, 28 far left; © xxmmxx/iStock.com, 135 (masking tape); © YekoPhotoStudio/iStock.com, 103 (broccoli)

Storey books are available at special discounts when purchased in bulk for premiums and sales promotions as well as for fundraising or educational use. Special editions or book excerpts can also be created to specification. For details, please call 800-827-8673, or send an email to sales@storey.com.

Storey Publishing
210 MASS MoCA Way
North Adams, MA 01247
storey.com

Printed in Singapore by Imago
10 9 8 7 6 5 4 3 2 1

Library of Congress Cataloging-in-Publication Data

Names: Abrams, Marion, author. | Lay, Hilary Emerson, author.
Title: Art sparks : draw, paint, make, and get creative with 53 amazing projects! / by Marion Abrams & Hilary Emerson Lay.
Description: North Adams, MA : Storey Publishing, 2019. | Audience: Ages 6+. Identifiers: LCCN 2019012767 (print) | LCCN 2019012803 (ebook) | ISBN 9781635861198 (Ebook) | ISBN 9781635861181 (pbk. : alk. paper) | ISBN 9781635862119 (hardcover : alk. paper)
Subjects: LCSH: Handicraft--Juvenile literature.
Classification: LCC TT880 (ebook) | LCC TT880 .A27 2019 (print) | DDC 745.5—dc23
LC record available at https://lccn.loc.gov/2019012767

DEDICATED TO THE
CREATIVE SPIRIT
WITHIN EVERY CHILD
(AND GROWN-UP).

CONTENTS

5 ART & NATURE

6 SCULPTURE

WELCOME TO OUR STUDiO

Hello! We love making art and we are very excited to share some of our favorite projects with you.

All of the projects in this book come from our Summer Art Barn camp. We spend all day going from project to project and letting our campers try out lots of different kinds of art. There's drawing and painting, of course, but also sculpture and working with fabric, paper, and nature to create beautiful and unique projects. At our camp we nurture creativity and encourage experiencing the joy of making art.

This book includes our very favorite projects so that you can join the fun. We give you easy-to-follow directions that show you how to use a variety of materials — most of which you may already know about and some you may not. We hope that these projects spark your imagination!

Each project will take between 30 and 90 minutes to complete. Our handy 1-, 2-, and 3-scissor icons quickly show you how difficult each activity is. On even the simplest projects, there's a lot of room for you to add your own touches and make it your own. We hope you try something new with every creation.

Hi! I'm Marion

and I'm Hilary!

NICE TO MEET YOU!

Marion started Summer Art Barn in 1989 so she could spend time creating art with her daughter, Olivia, and Olivia's friends. The program has become a popular creativity camp that enrolls 25 kids a week for the whole summer.

Hilary joined Summer Art Barn in 2013. She's a working artist who, among other things, paints pictures of animals wearing hats and makes tiny whimsical houses. She also makes funny monsters out of socks. (And you can, too! See page 98 to learn how.)

Good luck, and happy art-making!

Marion + HILARY

SETTING UP YOUR STUDIO

There are a few basic supplies you will need to complete many of the projects in this book. The good news is that none of them are very expensive — and some of them are even free. You can easily find all of the following items at your local arts and crafts store, or you can order them online.

Low-temperature hot glue gun

Make sure you have adult supervision when working with a hot glue gun.

Paper

Read more about paper on page 49.

White glue

Tacky glue

Toothpicks

are great for applying small bits of glue.

ELMER'S
Glue·All
MULTI-PURPOSE GLUE
For Household Repairs,
Craft Projects,
& more!

Extra
Strong
Formula
Dries Fast
Safe & Non-Toxic

4 fl oz
(118 mL)

Aleene's
ORIGINAL

ORIGINAL
TACKY
GLUE

★America's Favorite
CRAFT GLUE™

Premium All-Purpose Adhesive

8 fl oz (236 mL)

Found and recycled objects

Good paintbrushes

Read more about paintbrushes on page 15.

Paint

Read more about paint on page 14.

Black permanent markers

such as Sharpies, with fine and ultrafine tips.

Glue stick

clear or purple (which dries clear)

Good pencil sharpener

Pencils, including colored pencils

Erasers

9

FREE ART SUPPLIES!

There are a lot of ways to get free art supplies. Here are some of our favorites:

- **Go to yard sales.** What you find will likely be almost — if not totally — free.

- **Save tissue paper and ribbon** when you go to birthday parties.

- **Collect containers** for paint water.

- **Recycle** bottle caps, Styrofoam, and old toys.

- **Ask your local library** if they're throwing away any old books or magazines.

- **Take a walk!** Outside, you can find lots of natural things you can use for art, including interesting sticks, acorns, shells, pinecones, and stones.

- **Ask for art supplies** as gifts for your birthday and the holidays.

BE ART SMART!

We hope the projects in this book give you hours and hours of fun. Here are some tips to help make sure your crafting is as safe and successful as possible.

- **Set up a work space** — and cover it with newspaper or scrap paper if the project you're making is messy.

- **Gather everything** you'll need *before* you start making a project.

- **Always ask an adult** if it's okay for you to use a hot glue gun.

- **Clean up** when you're finished. Taking care of your supplies is a very important part of being an artist.

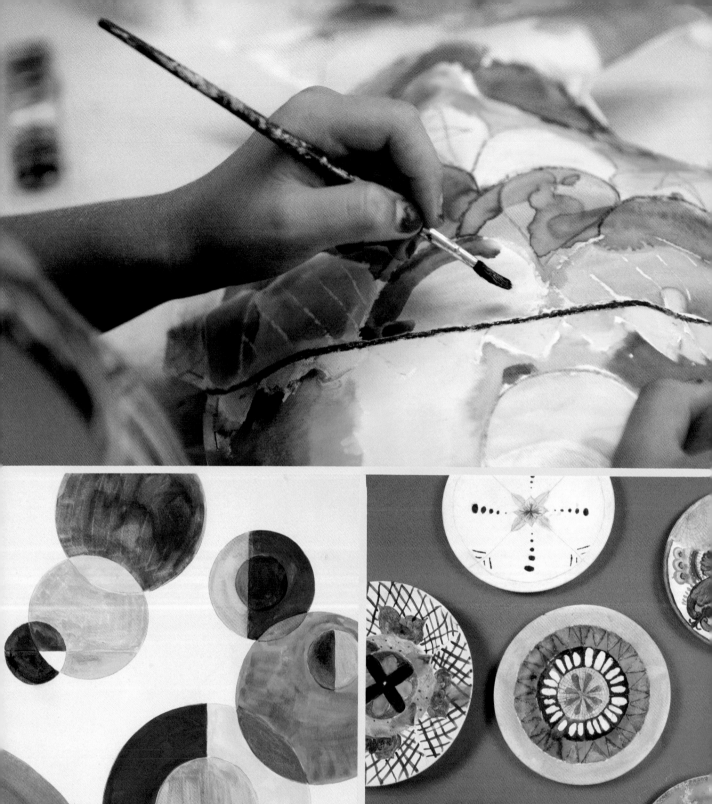

1

PAINTING

When you think of painting, you probably think of an artist painting on an easel. But in this chapter, you're going to paint on paper bags and dinner plates. You'll even paint with pencil erasers!

GET READY TO *PAINT!

Every artist needs some basic materials for painting. Here are the ones we will use most often:

Tempera cakes

KINDS OF PAINT

Watercolor in pans

These make colors that are *transparent*, which means you can see through the paint.

Liquid tempera

Tempera and acrylic paints make colors that are *opaque* (oh-PAYK), which means you cannot see through the paint.

Liquid acrylic

Also called "craft paint."

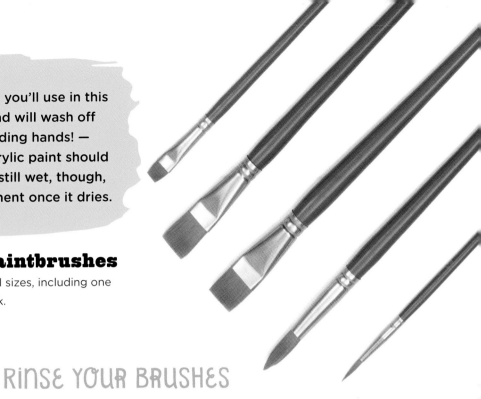

FYI All of the paints you'll use in this book are water based and will wash off of most surfaces — including hands! — with soap and water. Acrylic paint should be washed off while it's still wet, though, since it becomes permanent once it dries.

Pointed and flat paintbrushes

You should have brushes in several sizes, including one small pointed brush for detail work.

RINSE YOUR BRUSHES

As soon as you're done painting, wash your brushes with soap and water until the water runs clear. Then store them with the handle end down or store flat.

SURFACES TO PAINT ON

Heavyweight and mixed media paper

See page 45 for more details about different kinds of paper.

Canvas

You can buy prestretched canvas at any arts and crafts store.

Get creative

Projects in this chapter will get you painting things you never thought you could paint on. Paper bags? Plates? Rocks? Why not?!

PAINTING
NEGATIVE SPACE

Usually when you paint something you've drawn, you paint the object, right? In this project, you'll paint everything *except* the object! The space in between the objects is called *negative space*.

WHAT YOU'LL NEED

- Something to trace (like a pair of scissors or a cookie cutter)

- Mixed media or watercolor paper

- Pencil

- Paint (any kind)

- 2 flat paintbrushes, one large and one small*

*FYI Flat paint-brushes work best for this project.

1 Use the pencil to **trace your object** anywhere on the paper. Move the object to a different part of the paper and trace it again. And again.

Don't overlap your outlined shapes.

2 **Paint** every part of the paper *except* for the shapes you've traced. Use the larger paintbrush for the areas with more open space and the smaller paintbrush for tighter areas.

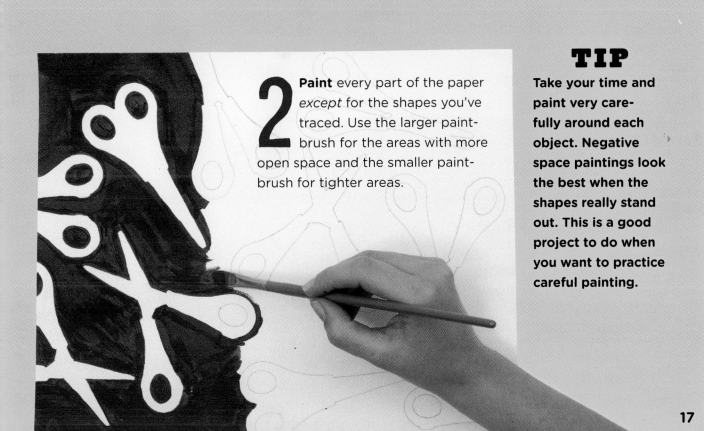

TIP

Take your time and paint very carefully around each object. Negative space paintings look the best when the shapes really stand out. This is a good project to do when you want to practice careful painting.

WHAT YOU'LL NEED

- 4 small sheets of heavyweight or mixed media paper (5 inches x 8 inches or larger)

- Paints of your choice and a paintbrush

- Pencil

- Scissors

- Large sheet of medium- to heavyweight or construc- tion paper for the background (9 inches x 12 inches or larger)

- White glue or glue stick

FRUIT & FLOWER COLLAGE

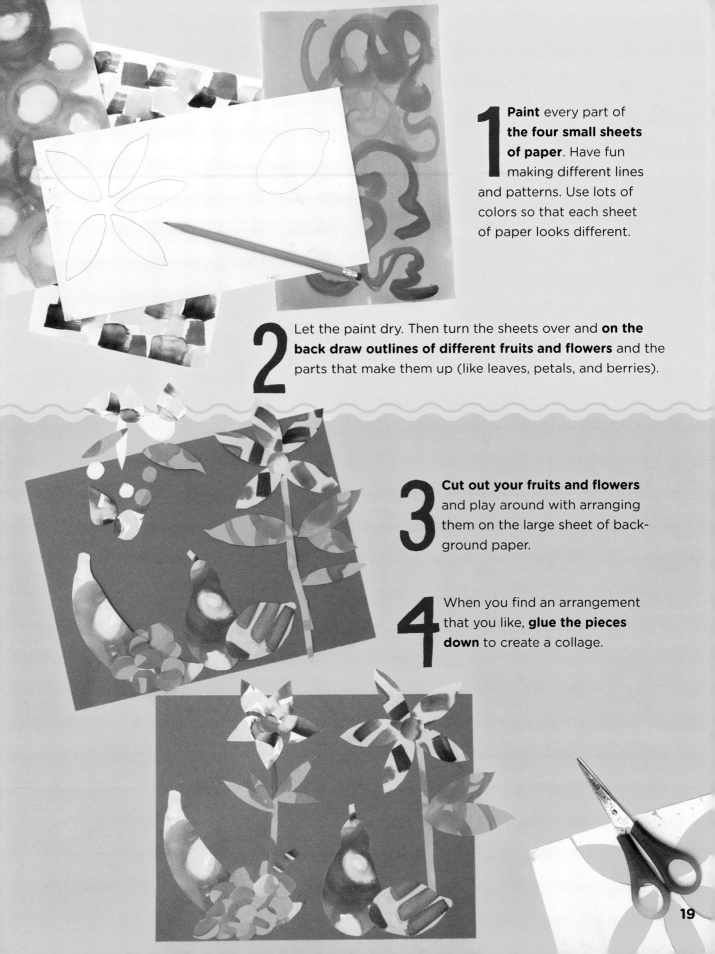

1 **Paint** every part of **the four small sheets of paper**. Have fun making different lines and patterns. Use lots of colors so that each sheet of paper looks different.

2 Let the paint dry. Then turn the sheets over and **on the back draw outlines of different fruits and flowers** and the parts that make them up (like leaves, petals, and berries).

3 **Cut out your fruits and flowers** and play around with arranging them on the large sheet of background paper.

4 When you find an arrangement that you like, **glue the pieces down** to create a collage.

19

PENCIL-ERASER
*POiNTILLISM

Pointillism is a way of painting that uses tiny dots of paints rather than brush strokes to create a finished work of art. French artist Georges Seurat is famous for his pointillist paintings.

Georges Seurat

close-up detail

WHAT YOU'LL NEED

- Pencil (for drawing outline)

- 8-inch x 10-inch sheet of heavyweight or mixed media paper or a stretched canvas

- 6 colors of acrylic or liquid tempera paint

- Paper plate

- 6 pencils with unused erasers

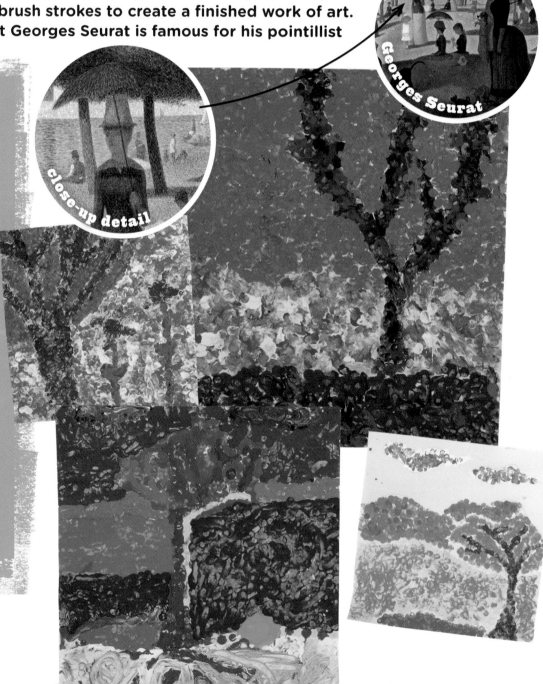

1 With your pencil, **draw a simple outline** of a landscape, a building, or any familiar shape.

2 **Place a little of each paint color onto the paper plate.** Make sure to keep the colors separated from each other.

Don't draw any details, just the outline.

3 **Dip a pencil eraser into one paint color**, **then dab it** onto the paper. Take your time and use this dotting method to fill in your drawing.

4 Let the paint dry and then **add dots in different colors**. This will give your painting a layered look.

- Masking tape
- Watercolor or mixed media paper
- Watercolor paints and a paintbrush
- Pencil and/ or permanent marker (optional)

TAPE-RESIST TREES

This project is easy to do and requires only a few supplies, but the results are beautiful. Plus, it's really fun to remove the tape and see the final result!

You can add details to your trees or landscape using pencil, a thin marker, or paint.

1 Tear up pieces of **masking tape** and stick them to your paper to make the shapes of trees and branches.

2 **Painting right over the tape,** paint a sky.

Make a snowy scene, a night scene, a sunset, or any scene you can imagine.

3 Let the paint dry, then **gently remove the tape.**

CIRCLES PAINTING

- Variety of round things to trace, in different sizes

- Pencil

- Large sheet of mixed media or watercolor paper (11 inches x 14 inches is a good size)

- Ruler

- Paints (any kind) and a paintbrush

TIP
Gather lots of round objects — such as a bowl, a roll of tape, and a plastic lid — from around your house.

1 Using your pencil, **trace different-size circles** onto your paper.

2 Use your ruler to **draw a straight line** down the middle of *some* of your circles.

Try overlapping some circles and putting a smaller circle (or two) inside of a larger circle.

3 Paint each **area** of your drawing.

Try blending two different paints to create even more colors.

AMATE BARK PAINTING

Amate (ah-MAH-tay) painting is Mexican folk art done on special paper made from tree bark. These beautiful paintings usually show colorful birds and flowers of Mexico.

WHAT YOU'LL NEED

- Scissors
- Brown paper grocery bag
- Pencil and eraser
- Fine-tipped black permanent marker
- Tempera or acrylic paint in white and 5 bright colors and a paintbrush

1 Cut the grocery bag along its seams. Use one of the large sides as your "amate paper." **Draw your picture** in pencil.

To make yours look like a real *amate* painting, draw fancy flowers with lots of leaves and birds with open wings and big, long tails. Your drawing doesn't have to look like *real* flowers and birds. You can make up your own!

White paint really stands out on the brown paper!

2 **Trace** your pencil lines with permanent marker. Carefully **paint in your drawing** but leave the background unpainted.

- Paintbrush (any kind, for the gesso)
- Old dinner plate
- Gesso*
- Pencil
- Watercolor or tempera paint and a small round paintbrush

OPTIONAL

- Ruler
- Something round to trace

*FYI Gesso (JEHS-soh) is a thick white mixture that artists use to prepare a surface to paint on.

Many places in the world, including Scandinavia, are famous for decorated dinner plates like this.

GESSOED *PAINTED *PLATE

It's really fun to paint on something other than just paper!

If you can still see the plate's original design showing through, paint on a second coat of gesso.

TIP

Ask your parents if there's an old plate you can paint on. If not, look for old plates at yard sales and thrift shops.

1 **Paint the front of the plate** with gesso. Let it dry completely.

2 Use your pencil to **lightly draw a design on the plate.** You can use a ruler to help make straight lines and trace something round to make a circle. Work slowly and carefully.

3 Using your watercolor or tempera paint and your small round brush, **paint your drawn design.**

Now that you've turned an old dinner plate into a beautiful work of art, **don't use it for food!**

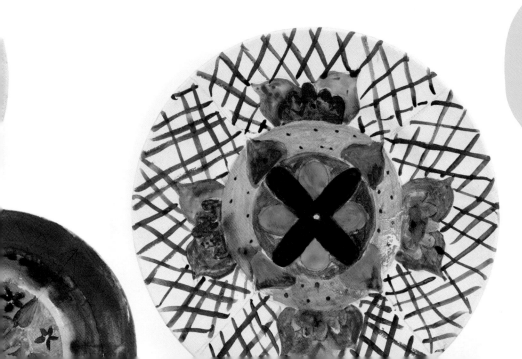

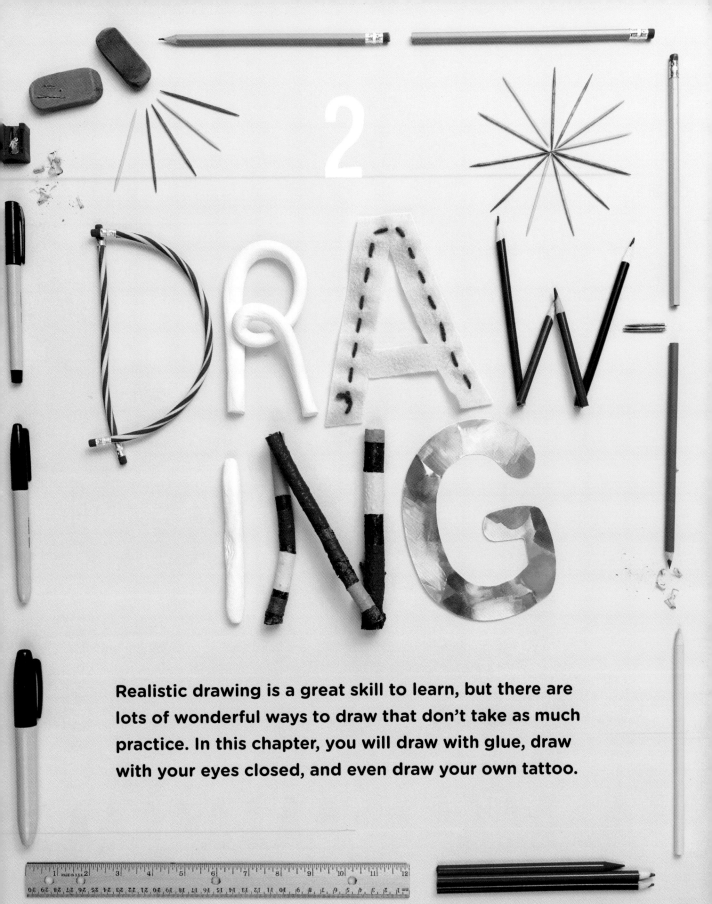

2

DRAWING

Realistic drawing is a great skill to learn, but there are lots of wonderful ways to draw that don't take as much practice. In this chapter, you will draw with glue, draw with your eyes closed, and even draw your own tattoo.

GET READY TO

DRAW!

Every artist needs some basic materials for drawing. Here are the ones we will use most often:

Pencils

Pencils come in different levels of hardness and softness. Number 2 pencils are in the middle of the hard-soft range and work well for all of the projects in this book.

Pencil sharpener

Eraser

A soft artist's eraser works better than the eraser at the end of a pencil, which can tear your paper. An artist's eraser can be vinyl, gum, or kneaded.

Permanent Markers

Permanent markers such as Sharpies come in lots of colors and tip thicknesses. In our projects, you'll use fine- and ultrafine-tipped markers.

Colored pencils

A set of at least 12 artist-quality colored pencils.

Crayons

Let's talk about paper. We use a lot of what we call "heavyweight paper," and we want to help you find the right kind of paper so that your projects turn out well.

On the front of most pads of art paper is a *paper weight* number. It tells you how much 500 sheets of that paper weighs. (So don't worry: that pad of drawing paper that says "80 lb." doesn't actually *weigh* 80 pounds!) The higher the paper weight, the thicker the paper.

A pad of paper that has a weight between 98 and 150 pounds is heavy enough that you can paint on it but thin enough that you can fold and cut it. It will probably say "watercolor," "mixed media," or "mix media" on the front. We recommend buying a pad that's 11 inches x 14 inches.

Did you know that lb. stands for pound and comes from the Latin word *libra*?

SKETCHING KIT

The best way to learn how to draw is by drawing whenever you get the chance. Put together a portable sketching kit: fill a tote with a sketchbook, a pencil, an artist's eraser, and a good pencil sharpener. Then take your kit with you when you go for a walk in the woods, when you go on vacation, or when you go pretty much anywhere else — and draw, draw, draw!

Paper
Read more about paper on page 49.

Oil pastels
These look like flat-tipped crayons, but they are softer and the colors come out brighter.

WHAT YOU'LL NEED

- Scrap paper or newspaper (optional)
- Pencil
- Sheet of heavy-weight or mixed media paper (at least 8½ inches x 11 inches)
- Colored pencils

TIP

Spread out several pieces of newspaper and lay your drawing paper on top. Your pencil may go off the drawing paper, so we want to make sure you don't draw on the table.

Do this fun, quick, and easy project anytime, anywhere!

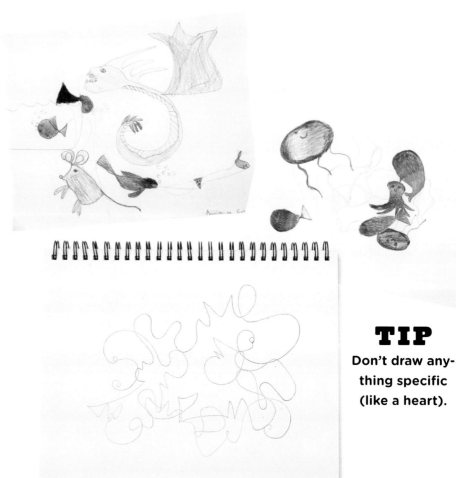

TIP

Don't draw anything specific (like a heart).

1 With your pencil on your drawing paper, **close your eyes and slowly start letting your hand follow your pencil.** Don't rush and don't scribble! Make loop-de-loops, zigzags, straight lines, and spirals. Open your eyes only once you feel like you've covered most of your sheet with interesting lines.

Maybe a certain curve looks like a head or a zigzag looks like teeth.

2 **Look at your doodle and find the monsters!** Bring each monster to life by making the outline a little darker with your pencil. You can add a few lines if you want to, but make sure you don't lose the shape of your doodle.

3 Use the colored pencils to **make your monster bright and colorful.** You should definitely add eyes. Maybe your monster also needs fins, wings, or feet?

Think you've found all the monsters? Think again! Turn your paper sideways and suddenly you have a whole new perspective. You may have 20 monsters in one picture!

ALUMiNUM FOiL RELiEF

WHAT YOU'LL NEED

- Pencil

- Piece of cardboard or foam core (about 6 inches x 9 inches)

- Blue gel glue or white glue

- Piece of aluminum foil 2 inches longer on each side than your cardboard

- Permanent markers in several colors

1 Make a simple pencil line drawing on your cardboard. **Trace the lines with glue.** Let the glue dry completely.

2 **Cover your cardboard with the aluminum foil,** shiny side up! Fold the foil around the cardboard. Rub the foil until you can see the shape of the glue lines.

shinier side

3 Leaving the ridges along the glue lines uncolored, use the markers to **color in the flat sections of your drawing**.

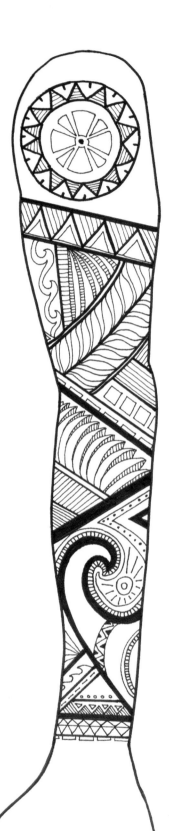

MAORi TATTOO

The *Maori* ("MAUW-ree") people are native to New Zealand. For hundreds of years they have passed down their stories and legends through carving, weaving, and a kind of tattooing called *tā moko* ("TAH moh-koh").

WHAT YOU'LL NEED

- Piece of heavy-weight or mixed media paper a little longer than your arm

- Pencil and eraser

- Someone to trace your arm

- Ruler (optional)

- Two permanent markers, with fine and ultrafine tips

1 Lay the paper on the edge of a table. Crouch down, and **place your arm as flat as you can** against the paper, spreading your fingers. Have a friend **trace around your arm with a pencil**, from your underarm down around your fingers and back up toward your underarm again.

Maori tattoos curl around the top of the shoulder, so use your pencil to draw a round shoulder.

2 **Cover every part of your paper arm with artwork** — even right down to the fingertips, if you want!

Maori tattoos use a combination of curving lines and straight lines. You can use a ruler to make your straight lines.

3 **Outline your arm** with the fine-tipped marker **and go over your pencil design** with the ultrafine-tipped marker.

To make thick black lines, take your fine-tipped marker again and color some of the open spaces black.

Each Maori tattoo tells a story about the person's family and important things the person has done. These beautiful and complex tattoos are traditionally done on the arms, the legs, and even on the face.

39

SHRiNK ART MASTERPiECE

WHAT YOU'LL NEED

- Shrink art sheet*
- Scissors
- Black-and-white drawing to trace (between 2 inches x 3 inches and 3 inches x 5 inches)
- Tape
- Sheet of paper
- Colored pencils
- Toaster oven
- Small piece of cardboard

OPTiONAL

- Hole punch
- Tacky glue
- Stiff, thick paper, also called *card stock*

People will wonder how you made these tiny masterpieces. The secret is special shrink art material that magically makes your drawing smaller!

*FYI You can find shrink art sheets at most arts and crafts stores or you can order them online. There are many kinds, so make sure you get the kind that is clear and presanded.

1 **Cut out a piece of shrink art sheet**, making it the same size as or slightly larger than the picture you're going to trace. **Slide the drawing** you're going to trace **under the shrink art sheet**.

2 On the scratchy side of the shrink art sheet, **use your colored pencils to trace and color in** your drawing.

Work carefully. You can't erase on shrink art sheets! To check what your work looks like, slide a piece of plain white paper under your shrink art sheet.

STRING IT UP

If you want to be able to hang your shrink art on a string, punch one or two holes at the top of your drawing after step 2 and before you put it in the toaster oven. Don't punch the holes too close to the edge. When your art has shrunk, you can put a string through the hole(s) and wear your piece as a necklace or hang it from your backpack zipper. You can also glue your tiny masterpiece on card stock, then hang it up!

3 **Bake your shrink art** in a toaster oven, following the directions that came with the shrink art sheets. Once your drawing has shrunk and is lying flat, have a grown-up **remove it from the toaster oven** and immediately **press the piece of cardboard** over the shrink art for a few seconds. This will make sure it's nice and flat.

Watch your art shrink! As it shrinks, it will curl up. (Don't worry. It will flatten itself out.)

WHAT YOU'LL NEED

- Mixed media or watercolor paper, cut into two 2-inch x 8-inch strips

- Mixed media or watercolor paper, cut into two 2-inch x 4-inch strips

- Ruler

- Pencil

- Watercolor paints and a paintbrush

- Fine-tipped permanent markers in several colors

- 4-inch x 4-inch piece of mirror board*

- Glue stick

- 8½-inch x 11-inch sheet of mixed media paper or card stock

- Scissors

*FYI Mirror board can be found in the scrapbooking section of most craft stores.

MEXICAN TILED MIRROR

Beautiful clay *Talavera* tiles are used throughout Mexico to decorate rooms inside many houses as well as the outside of buildings. Each tile is painted by hand, so no two are ever exactly the same.

1 Use your ruler to **draw lines 2 inches apart** across all four strips of paper. You now have 12 tile squares.

2 **Paint your strips of paper** with a very light layer of watercolor paint.

TIP

Use more water in your watercolor painting than you normally would, so that you can clearly see your pencil lines. If you use blue or green paint and the paint doesn't go on evenly, your paper tiles will look more like real Talavera tiles.

3 Once your paper is dry, it's time to **design your tiles**! Here's our trick for making all of your tiles look similar to one another: use your pencil to make a mark (like a small dot in the middle) on the first tile, then make that same mark on the rest of the tiles. Do the same with the next mark. Your design should look the same no matter which way you turn it.

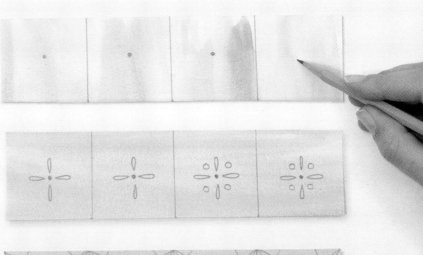

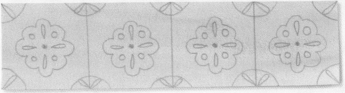

4 Keep going until you have drawn all of your tiles. When you work this way, your hand will remember how to make that same mark over and over again. **Color in the tiles** with fine-tipped permanent markers.

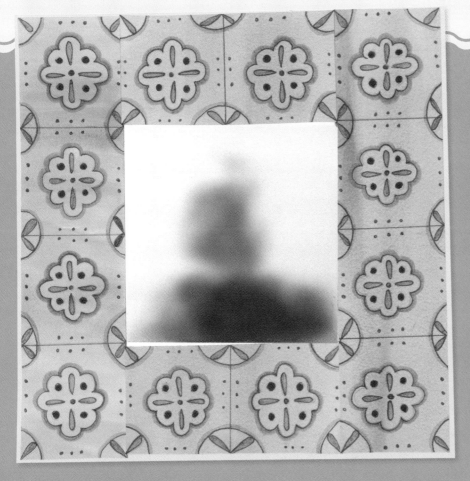

5 Glue the mirror board in the middle of the large sheet of paper, **then glue your tile strips** around the mirror board. Trim the background paper so that you have a little border around your tiles.

WHAT YOU'LL NEED

- Templates for *Movable Paper Animals* (page 174)

- Pencil

- Sheet of heavy-weight or mixed media paper

- Colored pencils

- Scissors

- Needle or thumbtack

- 4 tiny brads* for each animal

*FYI Tiny brads can be found in the scrapbooking section of most arts and crafts stores.

MOVABLE *PAPER ANiMALS

Have you ever drawn an animal that you can move around?!

If you trace as close as you can to the edge of the paper, you can fit all three animals on a single 8½-inch x 11-inch sheet.

1 Use your pencil to **trace the animal templates** of your choice onto the sheet of paper.

2 **Color every part of your animal** with colored pencils. Make it as realistic, or as silly, as you want!

3 Carefully **cut out the pieces of your animal.**

4 **Make a small dot on each piece of your animal.** Then have a grown-up poke through the paper with the needle.

TIP

The dots on the templates show you where the holes should be. Don't make the holes too close to the edges.

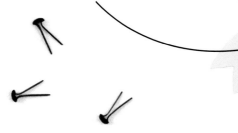

5 **Line up the holes in your animal pieces and, starting from the colored side, push each brad through.** Turn the animal over and spread the two ends of each brad apart.

3 PAPER ART

Almost every artist uses paper in some way or another. It comes in every color, thickness, texture, and pattern that you can think of. In this chapter, you'll discover all sorts of neat things you can make with paper — like jewelry, trading cards, and mobiles.

GET READY TO MAKE ART FROM *PAPER!*

Here are the materials you will use most often in the projects in this chapter:

Scissors

Mod Podge

This comes in many varieties. For paper projects, choose **Gloss** (shiny) or **Matte** (not shiny).

White glue

Glue stick

KINDS OF PAPER

Decorative paper

A paper with a pattern printed on one side, including wrapping paper and scrapbook paper.

Origami paper

A special kind of decorative Japanese paper that comes in squares.

Tissue paper

A very thin paper that comes in all colors.

Construction paper

A thicker paper that comes in all colors.

When Making Paper Art . . .

When you're cutting, instead of moving your scissors, hold your scissors straight up and down, then use your other hand to move the paper.

When you're gluing, spread the glue to the edges of the paper. This will help prevent the edges from popping up and ripping when you're finished.

When you're folding, make the crease crisp and neat. You can use your fingernail or the side of a round pen to press down on the fold.

WHAT YOU'LL NEED

- Tissue paper
- Mod Podge (or a half-and-half mix of white glue and water)
- Large paintbrush
- Sheet of heavy-weight or mixed media paper, cardboard, or foam core
- Decorative paper (optional)

TRY THIS

You can also use scraps of decorative paper with, or instead of, tissue paper.

TiSSUE PAPER PORTRAiT

Make an abstract portrait with lots of personality!

1 Tear off large pieces of tissue paper to **make the head and neck**. Use Mod Podge and the paintbrush to glue these pieces onto the sheet of heavyweight paper.

2 Tear up smaller scraps of tissue paper to **make the facial features**: eyes, nose, mouth, ears, eyebrows, and hair.

TIP

Don't worry if the tissue paper gets wrinkled or sticks up a little. That will make the finished project look even more interesting.

What else does your portrait need? A hat? A mustache? Earrings? A bird on top of the head?

✂

WHAT YOU'LL NEED

- Scissors
- Assorted pieces of decorative paper*
- Long rectangle of heavyweight, mixed media, or construction paper
- Glue stick

*FYI Buy decorative scrapbook papers at an arts and crafts store, or reuse wrapping paper, wallpaper, or any other interesting printed papers.

MAIN STREET COLLAGE

Make houses, churches, shops, or any other buildings that are on the main street of your town or city.

1 Cut out basic building shapes from your decorative papers. Arrange the buildings along your strip of paper until you like the way they look, and then glue them down.

TIP
Flip the decorative paper over and draw your shapes on the back before you cut them out.

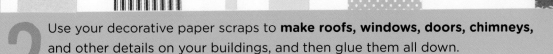

2 Use your decorative paper scraps to make roofs, windows, doors, chimneys, and other details on your buildings, and then glue them all down.

TRY THIS

When your main street is dry, you can carefully cut around the tops of each building, leaving a border about ¼-inch wide.

WHAT YOU'LL NEED

- About 12 pieces of heavyweight or mixed media paper (2½ inches x 3½ inches)

ARTiST TRADiNG CARDS

Artist trading cards are tiny works of art that artists send around the world through the mail.

There is only one rule for making these fun trading cards:

Every card has to be exactly 2½ inches x 3½ inches.

That's it! The rest is up to you!

After you have cut your pieces of paper, you can create all sorts of small masterpieces. Try using:

DRY MEDIA

Draw with colored pencils, crayons, pens, markers, pencils, or any combination of some or all of these.

Make a collage using scissors, images from old books and magazines, and a glue stick.

Have an ink pad and some stamps? Terrific! **Stamp** the card in an interesting pattern or use a pencil to turn your stamps into a drawing.

WET MEDIA

Paint with watercolor, tempera, or acrylic paints (using small brushes).

MIXED MEDIA

You can use wet *and* dry media on the same card. Try drawing a pattern with crayons and then see what happens when you paint over it with tempera paint. Or do a drawing with pen, then go over it with watercolor paint. You can use a permanent marker on a collage, a pencil over (dry) paint . . . Play around and have fun!

TRY THIS

You can do plenty of projects in this book on an artist trading card, including Doodlemonsters (page 34) or a Botanical Drawing (page 114).

STAR STREAMER

Star streamers are made for a popular Japanese festival, based on the story of a princess who fell in love with a farmer. The princess's father banished the couple from his kingdom and turned them into stars in the sky, separated by the Milky Way.

WHAT YOU'LL NEED

- At least 7 sheets of 3-inch x 3-inch origami paper
- Needle
- Sewing thread (about 1 yard)
- At least 7 beads
- Stick (about 1 foot long)

MAKE THE STARS

1 **Fold one square of paper in half** with the patterned side facing in. Unfold the paper, then fold it in half in the other direction, again with the patterned side facing in.

2 **Open the paper and turn it** so that the blank side is facing up. Fold your paper in half diagonally. Unfold it, then fold it in half diagonally again, in the other direction.

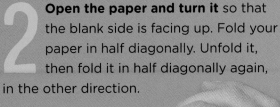

Make sure you crease all of your folds really well.

3 Lay the paper down with the patterned side facing up. Pinch two corners and gently push them together to **make a star shape**.

Repeat steps 1–3 with the rest of your papers so that you have a pile of stars.

continues on next page

HANG THE STARS

1 **Thread and knot the needle, then run it through one of the beads.** Bring the needle around and back through the bead one more time to secure it in place with thread.

2 Starting from the blank side of the paper, **run the needle and thread through the center of one of the stars**, and slide the star down the thread until it rests on the bead.

Repeat steps 1–2 with the rest of your beads and stars, leaving about 2 inches between each bead.

3 **Tie the star streamer** to your stick.

59

WHAT YOU'LL NEED

- Decorative paper
- Template for *Paper Bead* (page 175)
- Pencil
- Scissors
- Wooden skewer
- Glue stick
- Elastic cord* (about 10 inches for a bracelet and 2 feet for a necklace)

***FYI** You can get elastic cord at most craft stores. The 1-millimeter thickness works well for this project.

PAPER BEAD JEWELRY

Do you save interesting wrapping paper or other paper with neat patterns? Do you have some origami paper lying around? This project is a simple way to turn those fun papers into something you can wear!

TRY THIS

Paper bead necklaces look great if you string plastic or glass beads in between each paper bead. Or you can add charms — or even a finished Shrink Art Masterpiece from page 40, as shown above.

1 **Trace the template** on the back of your decorative paper as many times as you can without overlapping the lines. Cut out the shapes.

Make the most of your decorative paper by tracing close to the edge.

2 Starting at the wide end, **roll your cut-out piece tightly around the skewer**. Just before you get to the end, spread glue on the tip of the paper, then finish rolling up the paper.

Make sure the ends of the paper stay pressed down.

3 **Slide the bead off the skewer** and set it aside to dry.

Repeat steps 1–3 with the rest of your decorative papers.

4 **String your paper beads onto the elastic cord** and tie the ends to finish making a necklace or bracelet.

HANGiNG PAPER MOBiLE

WHAT YOU'LL NEED

- Decorative heavyweight paper, such as card stock or scrapbook paper

- Symmetrical objects to trace

- Pencil

- Scissors

- Glue stick

- Clothespins or paper clips

- Ribbon or twine

- Bead (optional)

TIP

Use simple, symmetrical geometric shapes like circles, squares, or triangles in your mobile. Look around you for things you can trace.

1 **Trace the same shape** on three different pieces of paper. **Cut out the shapes and fold** all three pieces in half the exact same way.

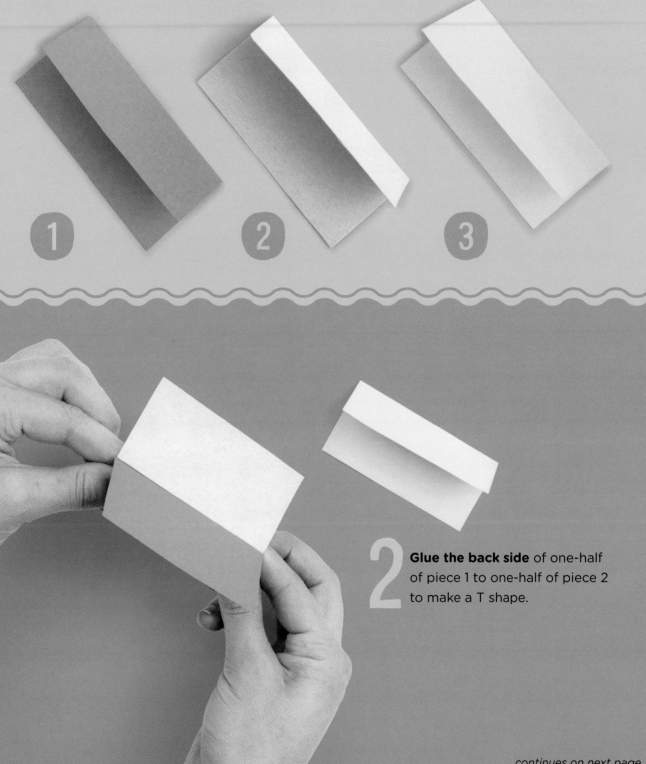

2 **Glue the back side** of one-half of piece 1 to one-half of piece 2 to make a T shape.

continues on next page **63**

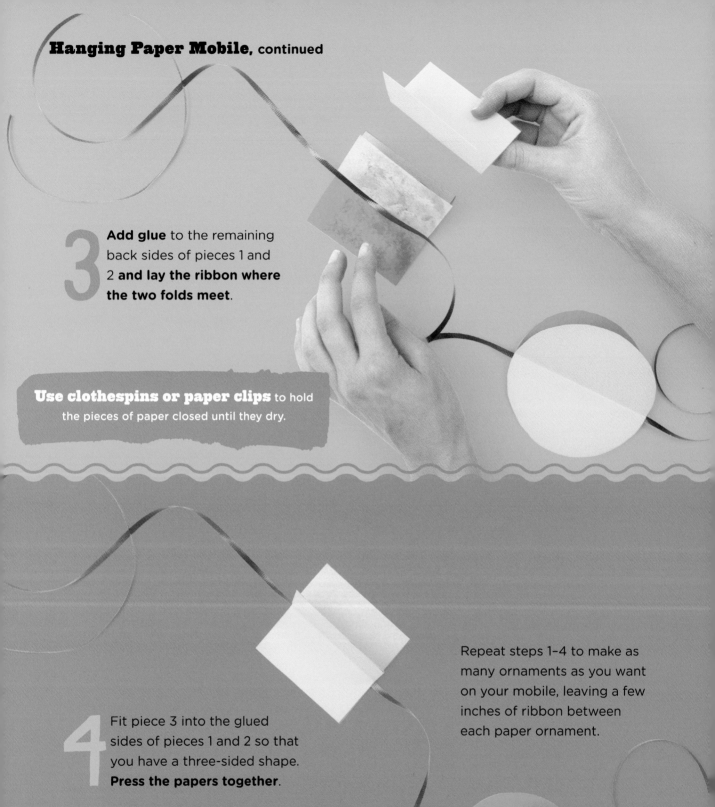

3 **Add glue** to the remaining back sides of pieces 1 and 2 **and lay the ribbon where the two folds meet**.

Use clothespins or paper clips to hold the pieces of paper closed until they dry.

4 Fit piece 3 into the glued sides of pieces 1 and 2 so that you have a three-sided shape. **Press the papers together**.

Repeat steps 1–4 to make as many ornaments as you want on your mobile, leaving a few inches of ribbon between each paper ornament.

WINDOW ART

These simple yet eye-catching mobiles look beautiful hung in a window! Tie a wooden bead at the bottom to add some weight to your hanging art.

WHAT YOU'LL NEED

- 6 sheets of construction paper (1 black sheet for the background, plus 5 brightly colored sheets for the shapes)

- Pencil

- Scissors

- Glue stick

*PAPER MOLA

The Guna women of Panama and Colombia use brightly colored cloth to sew beautiful layered patterns known as *molas*. You can make your own version out of paper.

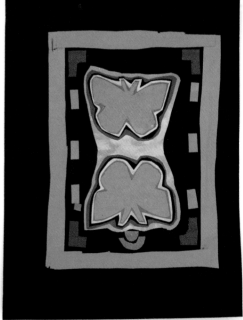

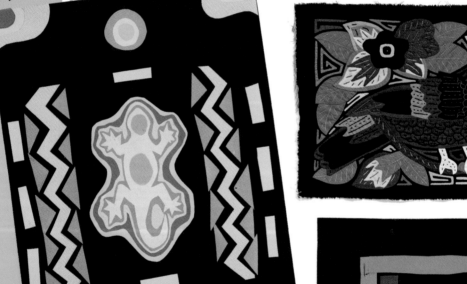

1 On one sheet of colored construction paper, **draw several simple shapes and cut them out**.

Your shapes should be **pretty simple.** Try making birds, fish, or flowers.

2 **Glue your shapes** (pencil side down) onto a different color sheet of paper. Leaving about a ¼-inch border around each shape, **cut them out.** Repeat this step to add a third color (if you want, you can add even more).

3 **Glue your layered shapes** onto the black paper.

You will have your original shapes plus at least two layers of color.

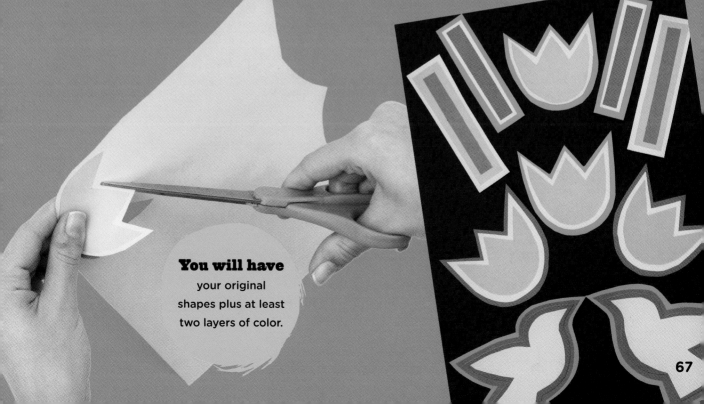

POSITIVE/ NEGATIVE

The curvy, seaweedy shapes in the collages of the famous artist Henri Matisse inspired this project.

WHAT YOU'LL NEED

- 4 small sheets of construction paper (4½ inches x 6 inches) in different colors

- Scissors

- Large sheet of construction paper (12 inches x 18 inches)

- Glue stick

Henri Matisse,
The Knife Thrower

You don't want ragged edges. Cut slowly and smoothly, being careful not to cut through any of the other sides as you go.

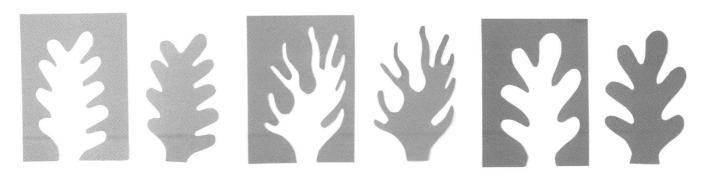

1 **Cut** into the shorter edge of a small sheet of construction paper, **turning the paper as you go to make a wavy shape**. End your cut on the same edge of the paper you started on.

2 **Repeat step 1** with the other three small sheets of construction paper.

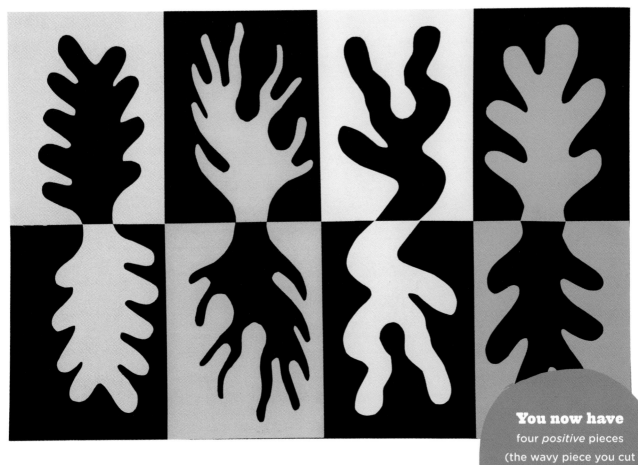

3 Arrange your eight papers on the large sheet of construction paper, **alternating positive and negative shapes on the top row**. Then match each piece with its other half on the bottom row. Glue down your shapes.

You now have four *positive* pieces (the wavy piece you cut out) and four *negative* pieces (the paper you cut it out of).

69

KIMONO DOLL

WHAT YOU'LL NEED

- 2 sheets of origami paper (at least 6 inches x 6 inches*****)

- Ruler

- Pencil

- Scissors

- Jumbo craft stick or a piece of stiff paper, cut to ½ inch x 6 inches

- Glue stick

- Small piece of heavyweight drawing paper

- Black ballpoint pen

- Magnet tape (optional)

*FYI Some origami paper is a little smaller than 6 inches x 6 inches. That's okay. Your kimono will just be a tiny bit shorter.

A *kimono* is a long, loose Japanese robe with wide sleeves. It is tied with a sash called an *obi*. Make them both with origami paper!

TRY THIS

Stick a little strip of magnet tape to the back of your kimono doll to make a fridge magnet!

1 **Measure and cut one piece of origami paper** to 4½ inches x 6 inches.

Make a very small fold (about ¼-inch wide) along the short side of the paper.

Turn the paper with the colorful side facing down and the folded edge at the top. **Lay the craft stick down the center** with about an inch sticking out above the paper.

2 **Fold each side** of the paper at an angle across the craft stick.

Then fold each side at an angle again.

3 Measure and cut your second piece of origami paper to 4½ inches x 4½ inches and keep one leftover strip. **Make the obi** by folding the leftover strip around the front of your doll and gluing the ends on the back. **Make the sleeves** by folding the 4½-inch square paper in half and gluing it across the doll's back. Trim the edges of the sleeves to shape them, if you want.

4 Use the pen to **draw a face** on the small piece of drawing paper.

Cut around the face and give it a nice long neck. Slide the neck inside the kimono and glue it to the craft stick. You don't need a lot of detail to have a lot of expression in the face! Try to draw a face in the style of traditional Japanese art, or draw in your own style.

4

FELT & FABRIC

Sewing is a useful skill to have (you can replace a missing button on your shirt or fix a hole in your jeans) but sewing can also be really creative (you can make a stuffed animal out of an old pair of socks or a hat out of a piece of felt). In this chapter, you'll make things to play with, things to cuddle with, and things you can use to decorate your room.

GET READY FOR FUN WITH FABRIC!

Here are the materials you will use most often in the projects in this chapter:

Fabric Scissors

You'll need a sharp pair of scissors that you use *just* for cutting fabric. Cutting paper makes scissor blades dull.

Tacky Glue

This is the best glue to use when working with felt and fabric because it is stickier and stronger than white glue.

Thread

You'll use sewing thread (which comes on a spool) and embroidery thread or floss (which is thicker, has multiple strands, and comes in little bundles).

Needle

Use the kind of hand-sewing needles called "sharps," with an eye big enough to fit embroidery thread or floss.

Chalk

Use chalk to trace templates onto fabric so you can brush off your lines after you cut out your shape.

Paint

Use acrylic paint or fabric paint to make fabric-based art. Both become permanent when they dry, which means you can put your fabric through the washing machine.

TIP

When it dries, acrylic paint becomes stiff, so it's best to use this type of paint for decorative items, and not for things you'll wear.

KINDS OF FABRIC

Felt

Traditionally felt fabric is made out of wool, but for these projects we use "craft felt," which is polyester.

Cotton

Most of your T-shirts and bedsheets are probably made out of cotton, which is one of the most common fabrics.

FYI For a few of the projects in this chapter, you can repurpose old pillowcases, bedsheets, or T-shirts.

Stitching

You can use just two basic stitches — the *whipstitch* and the *running stitch* — in all of the following projects.

To make a whipstitch, you "whip" the needle and thread around and around the edge of the fabric.

To make a running stitch, you pull the threaded needle up through the fabric and then push it back down through the fabric — over and over. It creates a dashed line.

- 4-inch x 11-inch piece of felt
- Embroidery needle
- Embroidery thread
- Stick (about 6 inches)
- Twine (at least 1 foot)

OPTIONAL

- Beads, with holes large enough for an embroidery needle
- Buttons

CHARM BAG

In many Native American tribes, healers carried charm bags made out of animal skin. They filled these bags with herbs, stones, feathers, and other objects they would use in their healing rituals. Make your own version out of felt and decorate it with beads and buttons.

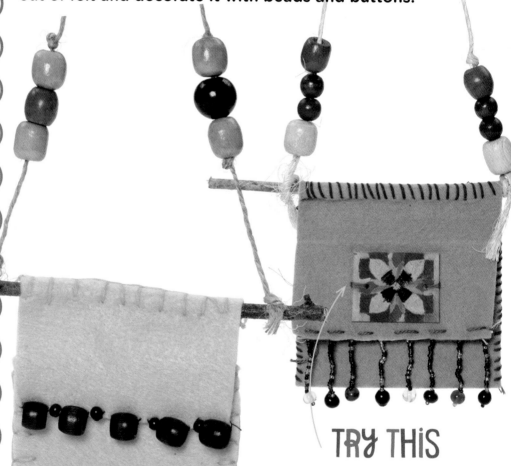

TRY THIS

Sew a button and/or beads — or a Shrink Art Masterpiece (page 40) — on the front flap to decorate your bag.

1 **Fold up** the bottom of the felt 4 inches **and sew together along both edges**.

4 inches

You can use any stitch you'd like, but a simple whipstitch (page 75) that goes around and around the edge works just fine.

2 Lay the stick where the flap folds over the pouch. **Sew the stick into place** by stitching around the stick.

3 If you'd like, **string some wooden beads** onto the twine, then tie the length of twine around each end of the stick.

WHAT YOU'LL NEED

- Felt, assorted colors
- Fabric scissors
- Needle and thread
- Bead or button

OPTIONAL

- Tacky glue
- Jewelry pin or hairclip
- Tree branch

FELT FLOWER

Don't throw away those leftover pieces of felt . . . they are flowers waiting to happen!

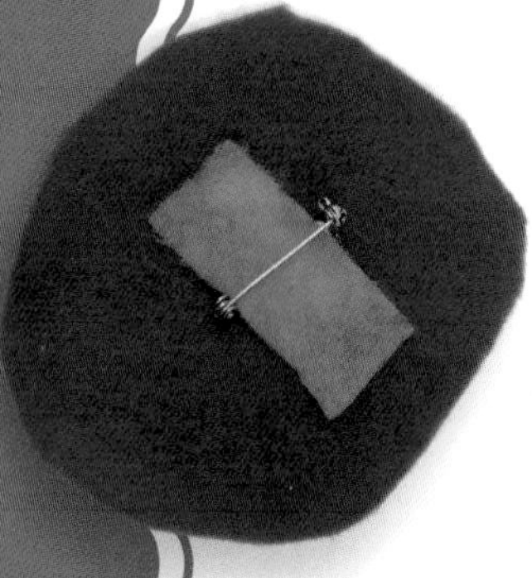

PIN IT

Using tacky glue, attach your flower to a pin or hair clip. Or glue it onto a tree branch. Or sew it or glue it onto a hat or a bag. Your choice!

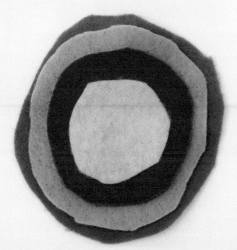

1 **Cut a circle of felt.** **Then cut out three or four more** felt circles, each one smaller than the one before so that they stack on top of one another in layers.

Your circle doesn't need to be any specific size or exactly round; these flowers look better when they're not perfect!

2 Using your needle and thread, **sew the bead to the center of your flower** through all the layers of felt.

Sew back and forth through the layers at least three times so that your bead and all the felt layers are secure. When you're done, knot the thread on the back of the flower.

- Felt, assorted colors
- Template for *Finger Puppet* (page 172)
- Chalk
- Fabric scissors
- Tacky glue
- Toothpicks
- Clothespins or paper clips
- Googly eyes, ribbon, yarn, mini pom-poms, sequins, feathers, and any other decorations you can think of!

FINGER PUPPET

Make a group of monsters, the characters from your favorite book, or a bunch of animals! The possibilities are endless.

1 Using chalk, **trace the template onto a piece of felt**. Cut it out. This is the body of your finger puppet. Use other pieces of felt to **cut out decorations for your puppet**, such as eyes, ears, and arms.

2 **Attach any details you want on the front or the back** of the finger puppet body using a toothpick and a dot of glue.

continues on next page

3 **Glue on any sticky-outy parts** (whatever you want to stick out from the sides of your finger puppet, like pointy ears or little waving arms) to the *inside* of the puppet body.

Put glue around the outer edges — but not the bottom — of your finger puppet, then fold it in half. Clamp the edges together with clothespins. Let the glue dry for about 30 minutes.

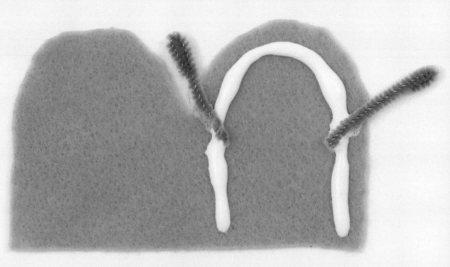

TIP

Make sure you don't glue shut the bottom of your finger puppet!

TRY THIS

Lots of details make your finger puppet truly unique. You may decide your puppet needs horns, a tail, a pair of pants, a soft round belly, or tiny freckles. Cut them out of felt, or add details with other materials. What about pipe cleaner antlers, yarn hair, or googly eyes? Maybe a sequined dress or a ribbon tail. Anything goes!

It's Showtime!

WHAT YOU'LL NEED

- Scrap paper or newspaper

- 5 pieces of white fabric, cut into rectangles about 5 inches x 8 inches

- Watercolor paints and a large paintbrush*

- Fine-tipped black permanent marker

- White or tacky glue

- String (about 2 yards)

*FYI Liquid watercolors, which come in bottles, are the easiest paint to use for this project, but you can also use watercolors that come in a pan. In that case, you'll need lots and lots of water to dilute the paint.

*PRAYER FLAGS

Colorful prayer flags are a part of Tibetan Buddhist culture. They are hung where the wind can carry their positive messages around the world. Traditional prayer flags are made in five colors: blue for the sky and space; white for the air and wind; red for fire; green for water; and yellow for the earth. Many prayer flags have images of horses, tigers, dragons, a sun and moon, the wind, and water. You can express your messages through pictures, words, or both.

1 Cover your workspace with scrap paper. **Paint one of your flags blue, one red, one green, and one yellow**. Leave one flag unpainted.

2 Let the paint dry, then **draw your pictures or messages** on them.

TIP
You can draw your pictures in pencil first before using the marker.

3 With your flags in this order — blue, white, red, green, and yellow — turn them over and lay the string across the top of each one. Leave a few inches between each flag. Apply a generous amount of glue to the top inch of each flag. Fold the flag tops over the string and press down to **glue your flags firmly to the string**. Wait until the glue is dry to hang up your flags.

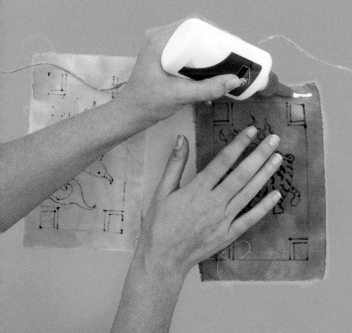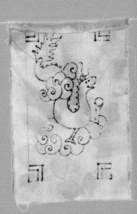

WHAT YOU'LL NEED

- Scrap paper or newspaper

- Styrofoam trays*

- Scissors

- Masking tape

- Acrylic paint or fabric paint in assorted colors and paintbrushes, 1 for each paint color

- Paper plates, 1 for each paint color

- Large piece of plain fabric, such as a pillowcase or a T-shirt

***FYI** Sometimes vegetables and meat at the grocery store come in Styrofoam trays. If you want to reuse a tray that held meat, wash it thoroughly with soap and hot water before using it in this project.

FABRIC PRINTING

You can print on just about any kind of fabric. Try making something new for your house or decorate a T-shirt that you can wear.

TIP

If you want to wash your printed fabric many times, use fabric paint. You can find fabric paint at an art supply or craft store, and follow the bottle instructions for how to use and wash the paint.

1 Cover your work space with scrap paper. **Cut some simple shapes** from a Styrofoam tray. Tape and pinch pieces of masking tape to make little handles on the backs of each shape.

Squares, rectangles, ovals, and zigzags are good shapes to make.

You can print **random designs** or make a pattern.

2 Lay your fabric out flat. Pour a small amount of each paint color onto a separate paper plate.

Holding your shapes by their handles, brush them with paint and **stamp them onto the fabric**. Let your fabric dry before moving it.

KUFi

A *kufi* is a short, round brimless hat originally from West Africa but now worn in countries around the world. Kufis come in many different colors and designs. Use felt to make your own.

WHAT YOU'LL NEED

- Chalk
- 7-inch diameter circle to trace around
- Enough felt to make a 7-inch circle and a 2½-inch x 24-inch strip
- Fabric scissors
- Ruler or yardstick
- Needle and thread or embroidery floss
- Straight pins
- Felt scraps
- Tacky glue

1 Using chalk, **trace a circle onto the felt** and cut it out.

TIP

Try using a plate, bowl, or a pot lid as the circle you trace.

2 **Measure and cut a strip of felt** 24 inches x 2½ inches.

You can also cut two strips of felt 12 inches x 2½ inches, then sew them together.

3 Have a friend **wrap the long strip of felt around your head** and pin it to the right size, with a 1½-inch overlap. You want it to feel comfortable — not too loose and not too tight. Cut off the extra felt. Use a running stitch (page 75) to sew around the ½-inch overlap to **secure your hat band**.

4 With the hat band inside out, pin the circle piece into the band. Use a running stitch to **sew the top of your hat to the band**.

5 Turn the hat right-side out. **Decorate the band** however you'd like using felt scraps and tacky glue.

MONSTER STUFFIE

Imagine a monster. It could be scary or friendly or silly — or anything else you want. Now bring to life the picture in your mind's eye!

WHAT YOU'LL NEED

- Felt, two 8½-inch x 11-inch pieces, plus assorted color scraps
- Fabric scissors
- Tacky glue
- Sharp needle
- Embroidery thread
- Fiberfill stuffing

TRY THIS

Give your monster a big personality. Is it tall, short, grumpy, friendly, funny? Maybe it has a moustache, or a long tail, or three eyes?! If you want to add other body parts, like a tail or wings, sew them on or attach them with tacky glue at the end!

TIP

Make sure your needle is sharp enough to sew through three layers of felt.

1 Use the two large pieces of felt for your monster's body. Stack the felt pieces together and **cut out the shape of your monster's body**.

2 Lay the pieces side by side; one piece is the front and one is the back. **Glue to one side** of the back piece **anything that will stick out of your monster** (such as arms, legs, tail, horns, or hair).

Use a small amount of glue about ¼ inch from the edge. The glue here is just to hold the felt detail in place while you sew.

3 When the glue is dry, **stack the front piece on top of the back piece**. Using a whipstitch and/or a running stitch (page 75), **sew around the edge** of your monster but leave about 4 inches unsewn.

4 Fill your monster with stuffing, then sew up the gap.

5 **Decorate your monster's front** using scraps of felt and tacky glue to add the details.

Stuffed with . . .

. . . **Personality**

FELT BiRD HANGiNG

This project is inspired by *bell totas*, which are hanging garlands of beads, bells, and brightly colored animals, often birds, made from fabric scraps. In northwestern India bell totas are hung by the front door to welcome guests into the home and to ward off bad spirits.

WHAT YOU'LL NEED

- At least three 8½-inch x 11-inch pieces of felt* in assorted colors, plus scraps

- Fabric scissors

- Templates for *Felt Bird Body* and *Felt Bird Wing* (page 172)

- Chalk

- Tacky glue

- Toothpick

- Ribbon (at least 3 feet)

- Small bell

- Sequins (optional)

FYI One 8½-inch x 11-inch piece of felt makes one bird.

TRY THIS

Traditional bell totas are sparkly and have lots of bells on them. You can use tacky glue and toothpicks to add sequins to your birds and ribbon.

94

1 Cut a piece of felt in half widthwise. Using chalk, **trace the bird template** onto a felt piece. **Cut it out**. Repeat with the other felt half so that you have two birds of the same color. Be sure to save the scraps!

2 Using chalk, **trace the wing template twice** onto scrap felt. Cut out both wings.

Using more felt scraps, **cut out another pair of wings a little smaller** than the first ones, and then one more pair of wings that are even smaller.

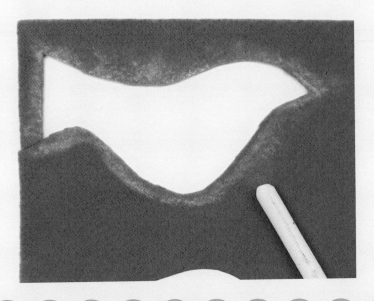

3 Lay the two bird shapes on the table facing each other. Using tacky glue and a toothpick, glue the biggest wings to the bird. Then **glue** the other **sets of wings on top so that they're layered largest to smallest.**

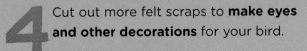

4 Cut out more felt scraps to **make eyes and other decorations** for your bird.

Use lots of colors!

5 Put aside your first bird to **let it dry.**

Repeat steps 1–4 for the other birds.

continues on next page **95**

6 **Once your birds are dry, attach them to the ribbon.** Lay one side of your first bird face down on the table. Put tacky glue around the edges and place the ribbon down the center. Press the other side of the bird down firmly to sandwich the ribbon in the middle.

7 Repeat step 6 with the rest of your birds, leaving about 5 inches of ribbon between each bird. Lay the garland flat so that it can dry.

8 When your mobile is finished, **tie the bell at the bottom of the ribbon**. Then tie a loop at the top and **hang it by your front door** to welcome friends and family!

SOCK CRITTER

Don't throw away those colorful stray socks . . . turn them into an adorable stuffed friend!

WHAT YOU'LL NEED

- Sewing needle and thread

- Fiberfill stuffing

- 2 (or more) buttons for eyes

- 2 socks (1 for the body and 1 for the arms and legs)*

- Ribbon or scraps of felt for clothes and/or accessories (optional)

- Fabric scissors

*FYI The longer the sock you use for arms and legs, the longer your critter's legs will be!

1 MAKE A CLEAN CUT

Lay the sock you're using for the body heel-side up. **Cut straight down the middle of the toe** and stop just before the heel.

Cut the other sock straight across right **above and right below the heel.** (You can throw away the heel.)

You just made the ears!

Then cut each piece in half the long way.

The piece where your toes would go in the sock will be the critter's arms and the piece that would be the top of the sock will be its legs.

continues on next page

2 GET IT TOGETHER

On the body sock, start at the top of one ear, and **sew down to the bottom of the cut and back up the other side**.

Sew up the open sides of the arms and legs, but make sure to leave one end open for the stuffing

Stuff the arms, legs, and body of your sock critter.

Sew the arms on the outside of the body.

Put the open end of the legs inside the bottom of your critter body and **sew the legs to the body**.

Your critter's legs are secured inside!

TIP

A whipstitch works well for this, but you can use whatever stitch you like best.

Sew on button eyes.

3 LOOKING GOOD!

Look for the sock heel that sticks out and pinch it together. Sew the pinched part shut to **make a fantastic sock critter mouth.**

All you need now is a name for your critter!

DRESS-UP TIME

Dress up your sock critter any way you want. A ribbon bow tie always looks nice, or you can use scraps of felt or fabric to make a little jacket or a dress. What about a hat? The possibilities are endless!

5 ART & NATURE

Nature has been an inspiration to artists ever since people began making art. In this chapter, you'll make some fantastic art using objects you can find right in your backyard (and even in your refrigerator!). Some projects use natural materials like pinecones and vegetables, while other projects are inspired by nature — like a field of wildflowers made out of tissue paper.

GET READY TO MAKE
NATURAL ART!

Here are some of the materials you can find in nature and use in the projects in this chapter:

Leaves

Make sure you know how to identify leaves you should avoid — like poison ivy.

Sticks

for these projects can be smooth or bumpy.

Rocks

Flowers

Pinecones

Before making art with pinecones you've found, make sure they're fully dry. Line a baking sheet with parchment paper and bake in the oven at 250 degrees Fahrenheit (120 degrees Celsius) for about 30 minutes.

Broccoli

Collecting Natural Objects and Using Them in Your Art

It's fun to walk outside and find things from nature that inspire you. Here are some tips to keep in mind when you do:

Take your time and look around so you don't miss anything.

Be respectful of rules and of other living creatures. Make sure you have permission to take things if you are in someone else's yard or a public space. Try not to disturb (and definitely don't take) anything that seems like an animal relies on it or lives in it — like an active bird's nest or a chrysalis.

Clean off what you find, if necessary, before you turn it into art.

WHAT YOU'LL NEED

- Smooth rock
- Acrylic paints and a tiny paintbrush

*PAINTED ANIMAL ROCK

The best rocks for this project are very smooth and about the size of your palm. The best place to find smooth rocks is near moving water (like the beach or a river).

1 **Paint the rock the main color** you want your animal to be.

2 Let the paint dry. Then **add details like eyes, ears, spots, stripes**, a white fur belly, feathers, or anything else you think your animal rock may need.

TRY THIS

Your animal doesn't need to be awake (a round rock is perfect for painting a sleeping cat) and it doesn't even need to look realistic. A pink hedgehog? Why not?!

You Rock!

ROCK COLLECTING

Now that you are an expert in painting animal rocks, you can start collecting rocks everywhere you go.

FABRiC LEAF TREE

✂

WHAT YOU'LL NEED

- Heavyweight or mixed media paper, foam core, or canvas (about 11 inches x 17 inches)

- Brown paint (tempera or acrylic) and a paintbrush

- Fabric scissors

- Fabric scraps

- White glue or glue stick

TIP

Look outside your window for inspiration. Notice how some trees are tall with branches at the very top and some trees are short with branches that start near the bottom. Of course you can also make up your own version of a tree!

1 On the heavyweight paper, **paint a tree with lots of branches** but no leaves. Let the paint dry.

2 While your tree is drying, **cut lots of leaf shapes and sizes** out of the fabric. Once the paint is dry, glue your leaves onto the tree branches.

You can make the same shape leaf again and again or you can make each leaf look different.

BRANCH OUT

Try making a whole fabric leaf forest. Or make a small tree on small paper with small leaves. These make cute greeting cards to send in the mail!

- Pinecone
- Sturdy stick (about 1 foot long)
- Masking tape
- Construction paper or heavyweight decorative paper such as card stock or scrapbook paper
- Scissors
- White glue
- Green ribbon
- Glitter (optional; use eco-friendly)

*PINECONE FLOWER

These pretty flowers will last forever!

TRY THIS

Add some extra dazzle to your pinecone flowers! Dab a tiny amount of glue on the ends of each petal and sprinkle on some glitter.

1 **Attach the pinecone** bottom **to the end of the stick** using masking tape.

To really hold it together, tape up and down as well as around and around.

2 **Cut out lots of pretty flower petals** from your paper. Dab a bit of glue to the bottom of each petal and **stick the petals into the pinecone.**

Liven up your flower by gluing on some paper leaves.

3 Apply glue around the masking tape and then carefully wind the green ribbon around it to look like a stem. Add construction-paper leaves if you like.

111

- Scrap paper or newspaper (optional)

- Several smooth sticks

- Acrylic or liquid tempera paint* and paintbrushes in various sizes

*FYI Having a variety of paint colors is nice, but if you only have red, yellow, blue, and white, you can mix and make all sorts of great colors!

*PAINTED STICK

There aren't really any rules for this project, but here are some of the things you can try:

- Leave part of the stick unpainted.

- Paint a stick using only dots or stripes.

- Blend colors into one another.

- Paint one side one color and the other side another color.

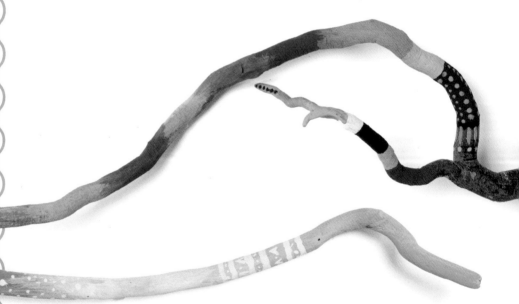

TIP

Lay scrap paper on the table so that you have enough space to paint and to set your branches aside to dry.

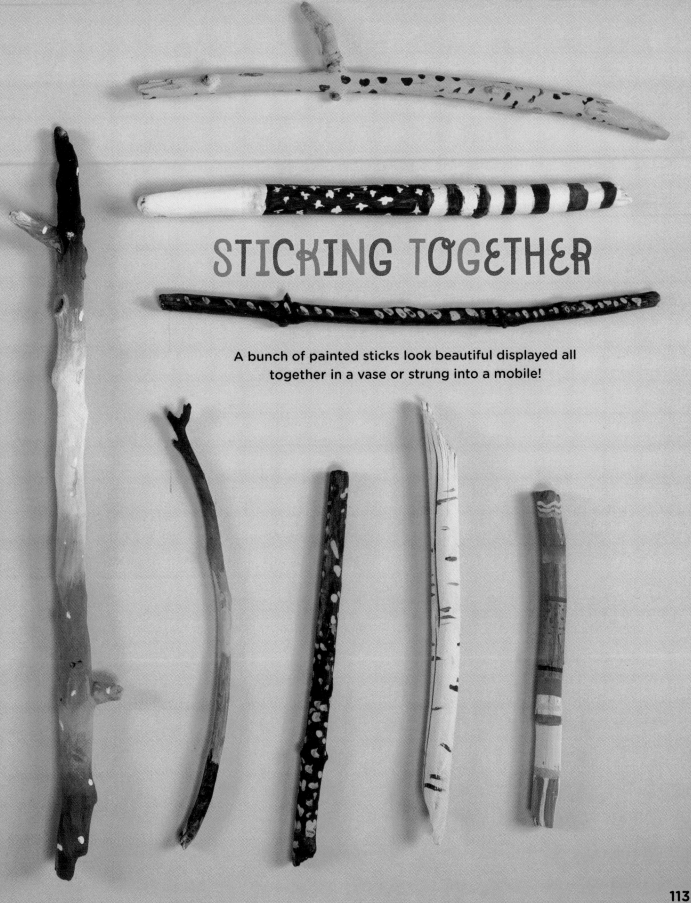

STICKING TOGETHER

A bunch of painted sticks look beautiful displayed all together in a vase or strung into a mobile!

113

BOTANICAL DRAWING

Artists have been creating realistic illustrations of plants for thousands of years. The oldest one dates back more than 2,500 years ago! Before cameras were invented, people used botanical drawings to share important information about plants.

WHAT YOU'LL NEED

- Flower or plant clipping

- Sheet of heavyweight or mixed media paper

- Pencil and eraser

- Colored pencils or watercolor paints and a paintbrush

- Glass of water (optional)

1 Use your pencil to **sketch the flower or plant**. You don't have to do any shading or draw in any details.

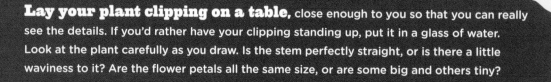

Lay your plant clipping on a table, close enough to you so that you can really see the details. If you'd rather have your clipping standing up, put it in a glass of water. Look at the plant carefully as you draw. Is the stem perfectly straight, or is there a little waviness to it? Are the flower petals all the same size, or are some big and others tiny?

2 Use colored pencils or watercolor paints to **color your drawing**.

Zinnia
Zinnia Elegans

Study your plant closely. That red petal probably isn't just red! It may have some orange or pink in it, too.

SCIENTIFIC SKETCH

Traditional botanical drawings have the name of the plant in fancy cursive writing, with the scientific name in Latin underneath. It's fun to look up these scientific names and include them in your drawing.

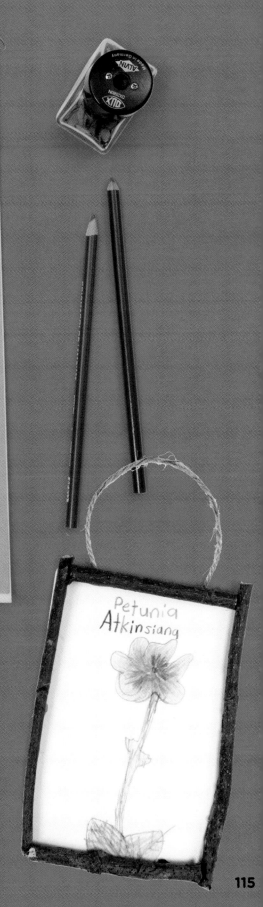

Petunia
Atkinsiana

WILD- FLOWER FiELD

TIP

If you made your field on a piece of cardboard and it curls when it dries, put it under some heavy books for a few days to flatten it out.

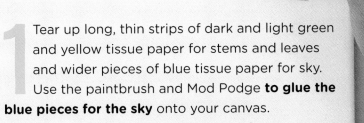

1 Tear up long, thin strips of dark and light green and yellow tissue paper for stems and leaves and wider pieces of blue tissue paper for sky. Use the paintbrush and Mod Podge **to glue the blue pieces for the sky** onto your canvas.

2 While the sky is drying, cut up other colors of tissue paper to make an assortment of beautiful flower blossoms and leaves. Use the paintbrush and Mod Podge to **glue down your stems, leaves, and flowers.** Paint another layer of Mod Podge over all the tissue pieces.

VEGGIE *PRiNTS

WHAT YOU'LL NEED

- Newspaper or scrap paper
- Paper to print on
- Firm, dry vegetables, cut by a grown-up to expose a flat side
- Acrylic paint and a paintbrush

Our favorite veggies to print with are cabbage, broccoli, peppers, mushrooms, celery heart, cauliflower, and apples. (Okay, we know apples are fruits, not vegetables, but they still work well for this project!) Try carrots and radishes, too — with the leafy tops still on.

You can make vegetable prints on lots of different kinds of papers. Blank notecards, brown craft paper, colored paper . . . experiment and have some fun! This project also works on fabric.

SHAPING UP

Vegetable prints look beautiful just as they are, but you may see some familiar shapes in your prints. The bottom of a bunch of celery could be flowers. A row of broccoli could be trees in a forest. A radish could be a balloon. If you feel inspired, grab a pencil, pen, permanent marker, or paintbrush and add some details!

celery

pepper

1 Cover your workspace with newspaper. Lay down a piece of printing paper. **Hold a vegetable** with the flat side facing up **and cover the whole surface in paint**.

If you're using a vegetable with leafy greens, paint the leafy parts, too.

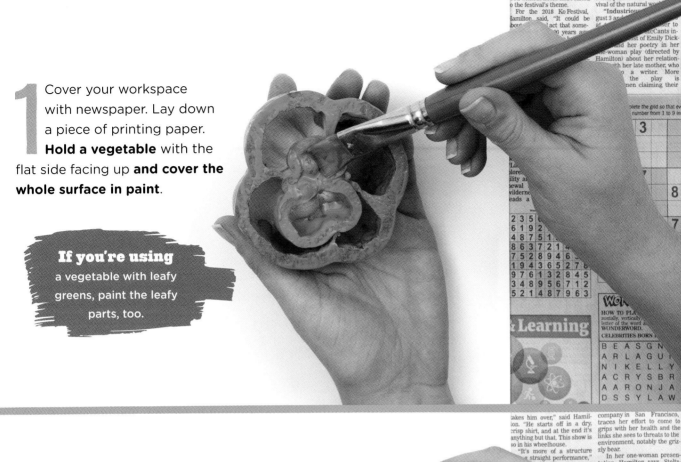

2 Carefully **turn your vegetable upside down and press it firmly onto your paper**. Gently press any leafy tops down with your fingertips and keep the vegetable from sliding around. Slowly lift the vegetable off the paper and admire your work!

TRY THIS

You can print the same vegetable over and over by reapplying the paint or by wiping it off and using a different color. Try painting the same vegetable a few different colors and see what happens.

WHAT YOU'LL NEED

- Paintbrush
- Piece of cardboard the size of the drawing you're framing
- White glue
- Drawing to frame
- 4 sticks
- Low-temperature hot glue gun
- Piece of twine or string

TWIG FRAME

Use this rustic frame for your Botanical Drawing (page 114), your Leaf Print (page 122), or any small drawing or painting you make.

1 Use the paintbrush to **cover the cardboard in white glue**. Press your drawing onto the cardboard and set it aside to dry.

2 **Have a grown-up cut the sticks** so that they match the four sides of your drawing.

3 Use the hot glue gun to **glue the sticks around the edges of your drawing** and to attach the two ends of the twine to the back of the frame, near the top.

WHAT YOU'LL NEED

- Scrap paper or newspaper

- Fresh leaves, with the stems on

- Acrylic paint

- Paintbrush

- A few pieces of paper to make the print on

- Several pieces of scrap paper

TIP

Try using several kinds of leaves, in various shapes and sizes.

You can also experiment with the kind of paper you print on. Blank greetings cards work well. So do drawing paper, printer paper . . . even a paper bag!

LEAF PRINT

The beauty of this project is that every single leaf print you do comes out a little differently!

DO IT AGAIN!

If you pick a sturdy leaf, you can repaint it with different colors and print it several times.

122

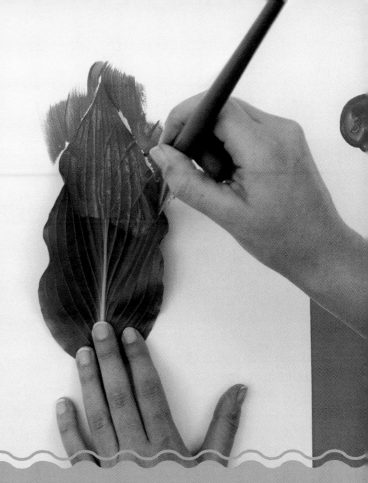

1 Cover your workspace in scrap paper. Lay a leaf upside down and **paint the back side of the leaf**, making sure you cover every part of it.

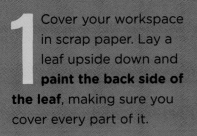

The back of a leaf is full of veins, which will make your print look really interesting.

2 Carefully **lay the leaf painted side down** onto your printing paper.

3 Cover your leaf with a clean piece of scrap paper, press down gently, and rub smoothly and evenly. Make sure you **smooth down every part of your leaf. Then lift off** the scrap paper and the leaf and voilà — you have a beautiful leaf print!

WHAT YOU'LL NEED

- Smooth stick (about 2 feet long)

- Yarn (any thickness) in yellow, red, white, green, and blue

- Scissors

- About 15 beads (with holes big enough for the yarn) in yellow, red, white, green, and blue

- Craft feather

TALKING STICK

Some Native American tribes in the Pacific Northwest have long used a special object called a *talking stick*. When members of the tribe meet in a group, the talking stick gets passed around, and only the person holding the stick can speak.

The five colors used in this project each symbolize something different: yellow represents the east, where the sun rises; red represents the west, where the sun sets; white represents the north and snow; green represents the south and the earth; and blue is a reminder that the Great Spirit will hear what is in your heart as well as what you say. In addition, the feather you'll use represents the courage to speak wisely and truthfully.

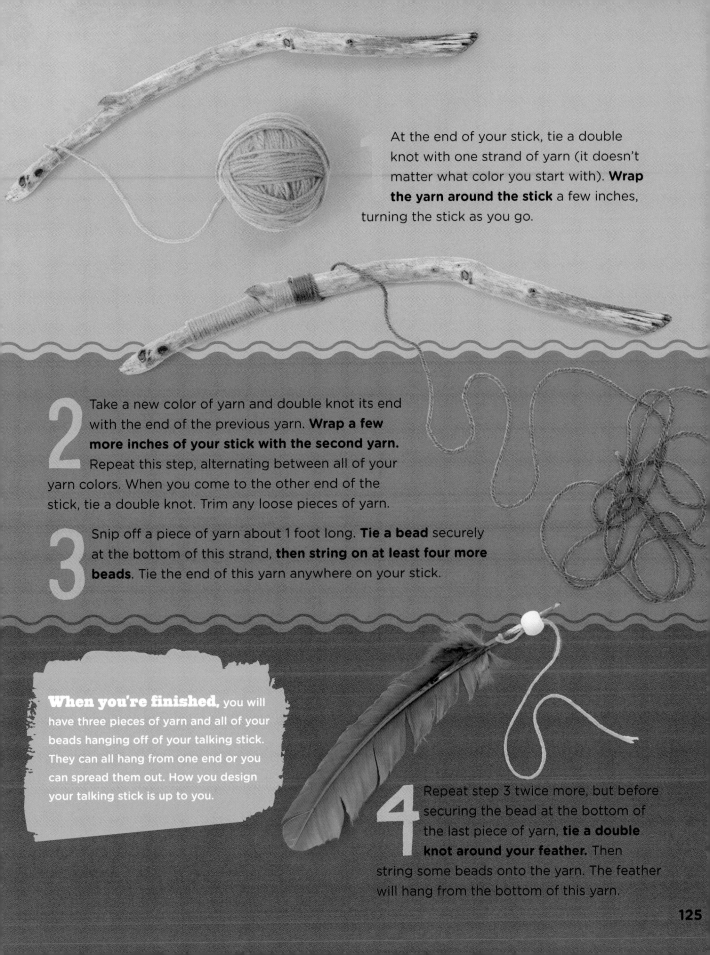

At the end of your stick, tie a double knot with one strand of yarn (it doesn't matter what color you start with). **Wrap the yarn around the stick** a few inches, turning the stick as you go.

2 Take a new color of yarn and double knot its end with the end of the previous yarn. **Wrap a few more inches of your stick with the second yarn.** Repeat this step, alternating between all of your yarn colors. When you come to the other end of the stick, tie a double knot. Trim any loose pieces of yarn.

3 Snip off a piece of yarn about 1 foot long. **Tie a bead** securely at the bottom of this strand, **then string on at least four more beads**. Tie the end of this yarn anywhere on your stick.

When you're finished, you will have three pieces of yarn and all of your beads hanging off of your talking stick. They can all hang from one end or you can spread them out. How you design your talking stick is up to you.

4 Repeat step 3 twice more, but before securing the bead at the bottom of the last piece of yarn, **tie a double knot around your feather.** Then string some beads onto the yarn. The feather will hang from the bottom of this yarn.

NATURE WEAVING

✂ ✂

WHAT YOU'LL NEED

- Tree branch shaped like a Y
- Yarn in various colors
- Scissors

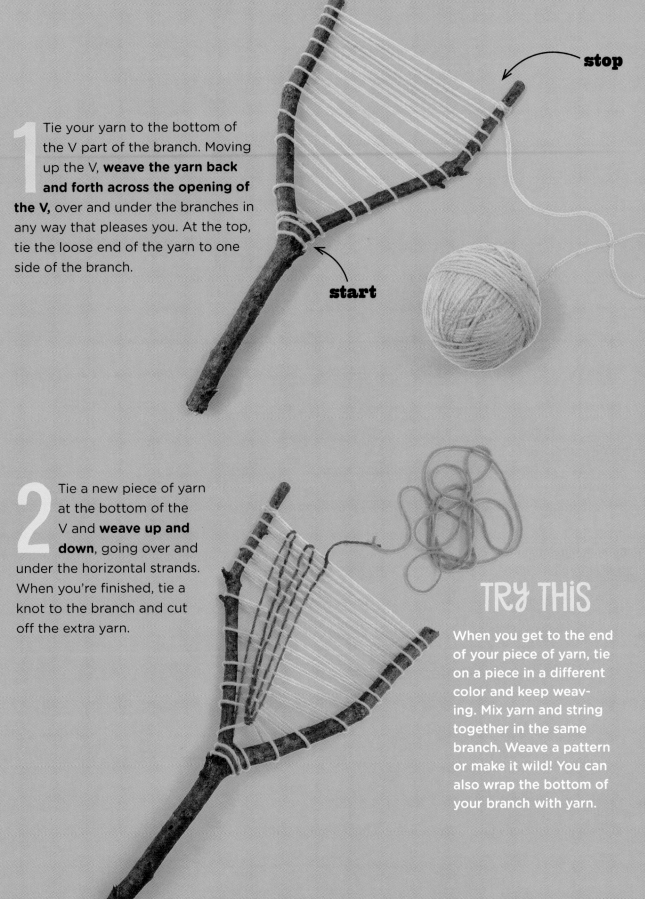

stop

1 Tie your yarn to the bottom of the V part of the branch. Moving up the V, **weave the yarn back and forth across the opening of the V,** over and under the branches in any way that pleases you. At the top, tie the loose end of the yarn to one side of the branch.

start

2 Tie a new piece of yarn at the bottom of the V and **weave up and down**, going over and under the horizontal strands. When you're finished, tie a knot to the branch and cut off the extra yarn.

TRY THIS

When you get to the end of your piece of yarn, tie on a piece in a different color and keep weaving. Mix yarn and string together in the same branch. Weave a pattern or make it wild! You can also wrap the bottom of your branch with yarn.

127

WHAT YOU'LL NEED

- At least 3 sheets of 8½-inch x 11-inch heavyweight or mixed media paper*

- Template for *Flying Bird Mobile* (page 175)

- Pencil

- Scissors

- Crayons

- Watercolor paints and a paintbrush

- Glue stick

- String or thin twine

- Paper clips

- Tree branch

***FYI** Each 8½-inch x 11-inch sheet of paper makes one bird.

FLYING BIRD MOBILE

Bring a little bit of the outdoors into your house!

HANGING OUT

It looks best when you hang the birds at different heights.

1 **Fold a sheet of drawing paper** in half the short way. Line up the bird template so that the bird's belly sits on the fold. **Trace the bird and cut it out.** Repeat with all of your sheets of paper.

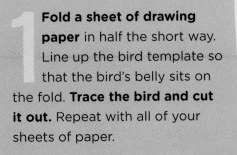

Make sure you don't cut along the belly; you want the bird to fold open as one piece.

2 Open up each of your bird cutouts and lay them flat on the table. Using crayons, **give your birds eyes, a beak, and feathers**.

3 When you've finished the crayon details, **use watercolors to paint your birds,** painting right over the crayon.

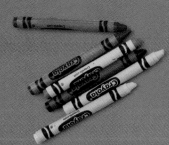

continues on next page **129**

Flying Bird Mobile, continued

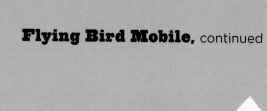

4 When the watercolors have dried, flip your bird cutouts over. On the blank sides, **use crayons to draw on *only* the wings.**

5 When you've finished the crayon details, **paint the wings with watercolor paints.** Set aside to dry.

6 Once your birds are completely dry, place them with the all-colorful sides facing down. Use the glue stick to **cover the uncolored parts of each bird's head, belly, and tail with glue.**

Don't glue the wings!

7 Lay a piece of string down the middle of each bird. **Fold each bird closed** so that it is glued together with the string coming out in between the wings. Press the sides together firmly. **Fold each wing down.**

8 Hold up the string and see how your bird hangs. **Adjust the string until your bird hangs straight**, and then use paper clips to hold it closed while it dries. Use string to hang your branch like a mobile, and then tie your birds onto the branch.

Your bird's wings should be free to flap up and down.

TIP
Look at a bird guide book to make yours look like a real bird (such as a blue jay or a robin) or create your own bird.

6

SCULPTURE

Artists make sculptures out of all sorts of materials, including stone, wood, glass, and wire. Some sculptures are small enough to fit in the palm of a hand, and some are large enough to fill a gymnasium. Luckily, you don't need special tools or materials to make an awesome sculpture. In this chapter, you'll make tiny toy people, giant animals, witches, and so much more from everyday objects like newspaper, cardboard, and bottles.

GET READY TO SCULPT*!

Here are some of the materials you will use in this chapter:

Kitchen Cupboard Basics

Your kitchen is full of great materials for making art.

Flour

Cream of Tartar

Clay

Artists use many kinds of clay. For projects in this chapter, you'll use self-hardening (or air-dry) clay, which comes in brown or white. You should finish each project in one sitting or else the clay will harden and you won't be able to shape it anymore.

Mod Podge

Newspaper

Masking Tape

Clothespins

Recycled Objects

Look for loose parts around your house and give them new life in your art!

Pipe cleaners

WHAT YOU'LL NEED

- Liquid acrylic paint
- 2 paintbrushes
- Clean, empty glass bottle
- Old magazines
- Scissors
- Mod Podge (or a half-and-half mix of white glue and water)
- Ribbon (optional)

TRY THIS

When your bottle is completely dry, you can finish it by tying a ribbon around the top.

FANCY DECOUPAGE BOTTLE

Decoupage ("day-coo-PAHJ") means "decorating by gluing on cutout pieces of paper." It comes from the French word *decouper*, which means "to cut."

HOLD IT!

Use your fancy bottle as a pencil holder or a vase (just make sure not to get the outside of the bottle wet).

TIP
Painting your bottle all one color works best for this project.

1 **Paint the bottle** heavily enough on the oustide so you can't see through it.

You may need two coats of paint.

2 While the paint dries, **cut out pictures from magazines**.

Maybe you want a theme for your bottle — like flowers, animals, ladies in fancy hats, or pictures that are all the same color. Or maybe you just want to cut out whichever pictures grab your attention.

3 When the paint is dry, use Mod Podge and the other paintbrush to **glue the pictures onto the bottle**. Paint a little Mod Podge onto the bottle, apply a picture, and paint another coat of Mod Podge over it. At the very end, cover your whole bottle with another coat of Mod Podge.

CLAY BEAN MANDALA

The word *mandala* means "circle." In both Hinduism and Buddhism, mandalas are spiritual symbols representing the universe. Some mandalas are done as drawings, some are paintings, and some are even made out of colorful sand. For this one, you'll use clay and beans.

1 **Pat the clay into a circle** about ½ inch thick and 5 inches across. Use a toothpick to **draw a square** big enough to touch the edges of the circle.

If you want your circle to be perfect, **trace a cup.**

2 Use the toothpick to **draw a circle inside the square** big enough to touch the sides of the square. **Firmly press beans into the clay** in an interesting, and balanced pattern.

3 Let your mandala dry for several days. Then **brush on a coat of Mod Podge** to make the clay stronger and help secure the beans. Put it aside to dry again.

✂ + a grown-up

WHAT YOU'LL NEED

- 2 cups flour
- 2 cups water
- ½ cup salt
- 2 tablespoons cream of tartar*
- Fork
- Saucepan

OPTIONAL

- Spoon
- Vegetable oil
- Acrylic or craft paint
- Paintbrush

FYI Cream of tartar is a white powder that you can find in the spice section of the grocery store.

HOME-MADE *PLAY ❀DOUGH

MAKE THE DOUGH

1 **Mix the flour, water, salt, and cream of tartar** with a fork in a saucepan. Cook it over low-to-medium heat, stirring with a spoon for about 5 minutes, until it starts to **form a ball**.

If it's too wet, add a little flour. If it's too dry, add a drop or two of vegetable oil.

2 Remove from the heat and let cool for 10 minutes. Once the mixture is cool, place it on a table and **knead it to form a smooth consistency**.

USE THE DOUGH

3 Gently **squeeze** a piece of dough **into the shape you want.** When you make something you want to keep, put it in a warm place to dry. After it hardens for a few days you can **paint it.**

TIP
If you store your homemade play dough in a sealed plastic bag, it will last for months.

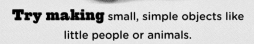

Try making small, simple objects like little people or animals.

- Fun stuff you've collected
- Low-temperature hot glue gun (for the larger pieces)
- Tacky glue (for the smaller pieces)

FOUND OBJECT SCULPTURE

This project starts with a treasure hunt. You'll gather interesting objects from around your house that inspire you.

SURROUNDED BY STUFF

Look around for interesting pieces of cardboard, packing materials, plastic containers, empty boxes, old toys, party favors, and knick-knacks. Ask a grown-up if they have any old costume jewelry or buttons they can donate to your sculpture.

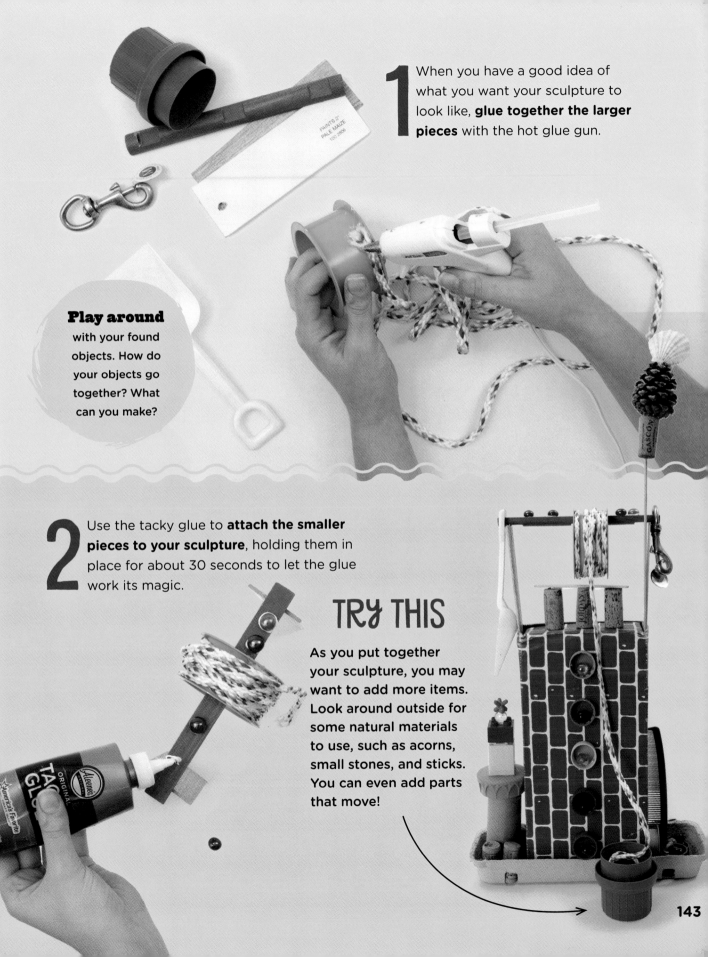

1 When you have a good idea of what you want your sculpture to look like, **glue together the larger pieces** with the hot glue gun.

Play around with your found objects. How do your objects go together? What can you make?

2 Use the tacky glue to **attach the smaller pieces to your sculpture**, holding them in place for about 30 seconds to let the glue work its magic.

TRY THIS

As you put together your sculpture, you may want to add more items. Look around outside for some natural materials to use, such as acorns, small stones, and sticks. You can even add parts that move!

143

WHAT YOU'LL NEED

- Pipe cleaners, cut 6-inches long

- One-piece wooden clothespins (not the kind that open and close)

- Masking tape

- Ultrafine-tipped black permanent marker

- Toothpick

- Tacky glue

- Fabric scraps

- Sharp scissors

- Ribbons, lace, felt, or yarn

- Piece of heavy card-board or wood, for a stand (optional)

CLOTHESPIN *PERSON

What kind of person will you make? One of your family members? A character from your favorite fairy tale? A fancy lady going to a ball? Someone on the way to the beach? You decide!

Play around with fabric scraps to see how you'd like to dress your person. Go casual with shorts and a T-shirt. Or old-fashioned with a dress and an apron. Maybe you're making a superhero and she needs a cape! What about a wand or a hat?! You can make fun accessories and props or even borrow them from an old toy.

1 To make the arms, **wrap the pipe cleaner around the clothespin**, twist it once in the back, and fold the ends toward the front. Use a small piece of tape to hold the arms in place.

2 **Draw a little face** using permanent marker. Use the toothpick and glue to **put clothes on your person, add hair**, and attach any other decorations you want.

TIP

Hold the fabric pieces in place for a few seconds to make sure they stick.

BIG & FANCY

Want to dress your clothespin person in a big, fancy gown? Use scrunched up newspaper and masking tape to make the dress form before adding fabric to the outside. Your person just might be able to stand up on her own!

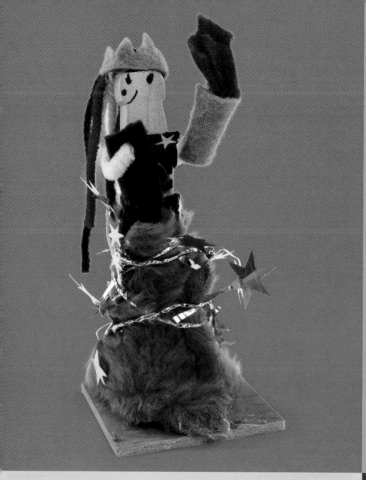

Stand Up

146

for Creativity!

TRY THIS

Use tacky glue and a piece of cardboard to make a stand. Some craft stores also sell little stands that will hold up your clothespin person.

- Styrofoam or news-paper ball (for head)

- Glass bottle

- Masking tape

- Pipe cleaner

- Craft paint

- Low-temperature hot glue gun or tacky glue

- 2 buttons (for eyes)

- Fabric and/or ribbon scraps

- Scissors

- Yarn (for hair)

OPTIONAL

- Template for *Kitchen Witch Hat* (page 173)

- Piece of black construction paper (for hat)

- Thin stick (for broom)

- Handful of straw or raffia, cut into 4-inch pieces, and string (for broom)

KiTCHEN WiTCH

Sweet little witches like these live in kitchens throughout Scandinavian countries, making sure pots don't boil over and food in the oven doesn't burn.

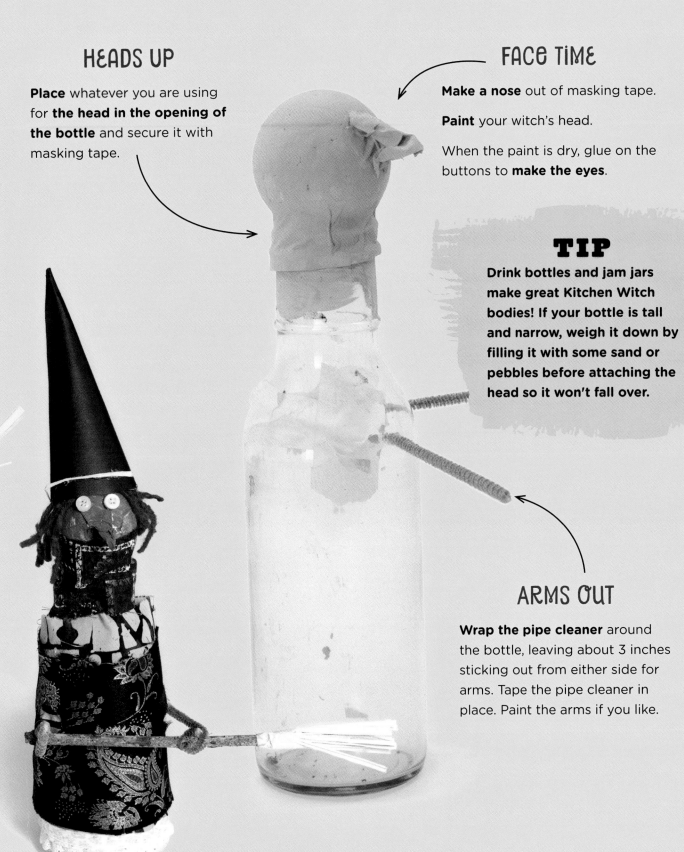

HEADS UP

Place whatever you are using for **the head in the opening of the bottle** and secure it with masking tape.

FACE TIME

Make a nose out of masking tape.

Paint your witch's head.

When the paint is dry, glue on the buttons to **make the eyes**.

TIP

Drink bottles and jam jars make great Kitchen Witch bodies! If your bottle is tall and narrow, weigh it down by filling it with some sand or pebbles before attaching the head so it won't fall over.

ARMS OUT

Wrap the pipe cleaner around the bottle, leaving about 3 inches sticking out from either side for arms. Tape the pipe cleaner in place. Paint the arms if you like.

continues on next page **149**

DRESS UP

Wrap a piece of fabric around the bottle to **make your witch's dress.** Secure the dress in place with a few dabs of glue on the back of the bottle.

HAIR DO

Glue the yarn hair to the top of your witch's head.

TIP

The fabric you use for the dress should be long enough to hide the bottom of the bottle. You can either cut little armholes from the fabric or wrap the fabric around your witch's arms.

WHAT TO WEAR

Use fabric scraps and/or ribbons to give your witch a creative outfit. Does she need a scarf? An apron? A cape?! Or dress your witch in old doll clothes. Don't limit yourself! Use found objects — like acorns or old jewelry — to decorate her outfit.

HAT

Trace both parts of the hat template onto the construction paper. Cut out both pieces. Roll the hat top into a cone and secure it with glue. Push the cone up through the hole in the brim as far as you can. Cut slits in the bottom of the cone. Add a tiny bit of glue to each slit and fold back to secure to the brim. Using glue, attach the hat to the witch's head. You can decorate the brim of the hat with ribbon or fabric if you'd like your witch to be even fancier.

BROOM

Use a piece of string or ribbon to tie the straw or raffia to the bottom of your stick. Curl one of the witch's arms around the broom to hold it.

Ta da!
You're finished!

WHAT YOU'LL NEED

- Tape or glue stick

- Templates for *Stuffed Fish* (pages 170–71)

- Pencil

- 2 sheets of mixed media paper (at least 11 inches x 17 inches)

- Scissors

- Crayons

- Watercolor paints and a paintbrush

- Stapler

- Fiberfill stuffing

- Hole punch

- Ribbon or string (at least 2 feet)

1 Tape or glue together the two parts of the template. Using the pencil, **trace the template** on two sheets of paper.

2 **Cut out your fish outlines** and place them on the table **so that they face each other.**

3 Use crayons to **draw the details** of your fish. Make sure it has big eyes, two fins, and lots of scales.

4 **Paint the entire fish with watercolor paints.** (The paint will bead up when you go over the crayon.)

TIP
Only decorate the face-up sides, not the sides facing the table.

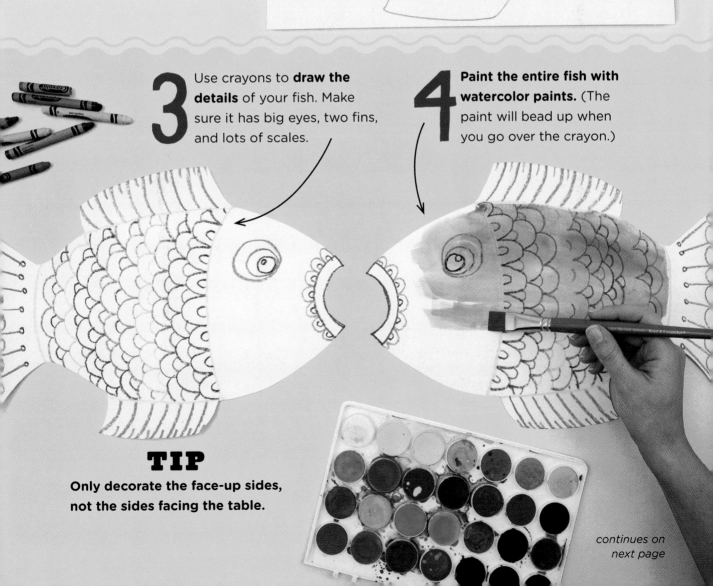

continues on next page

5 When the paint is dry, **match up both pieces of the fish**, with the decorated sides facing out.

6 Starting at the tail, **staple** together both pieces of the fish **around the outer edge**. After stapling some, **stuff the fish** with small pieces of stuffing.

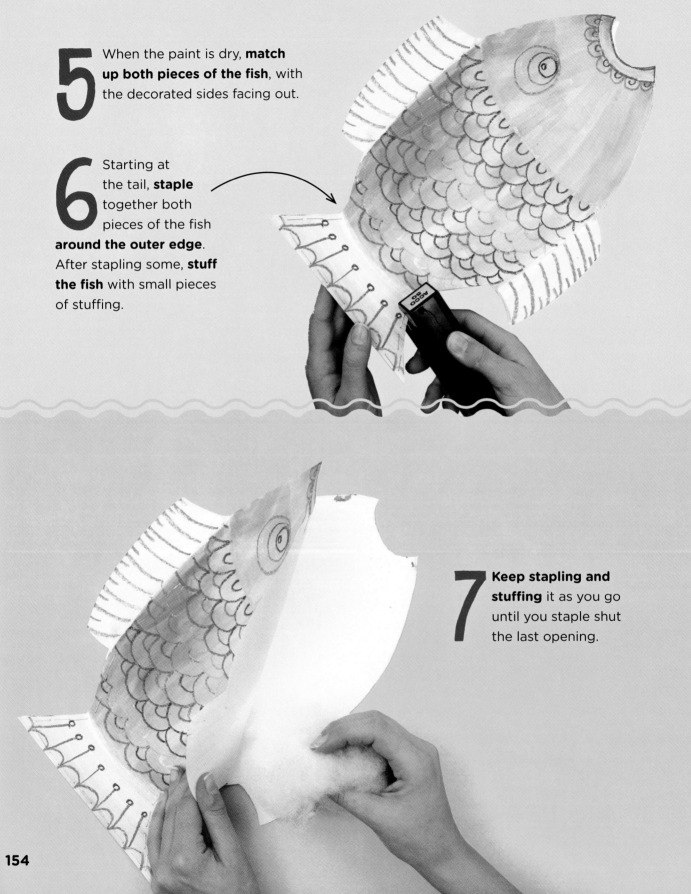

7 **Keep stapling and stuffing** it as you go until you staple shut the last opening.

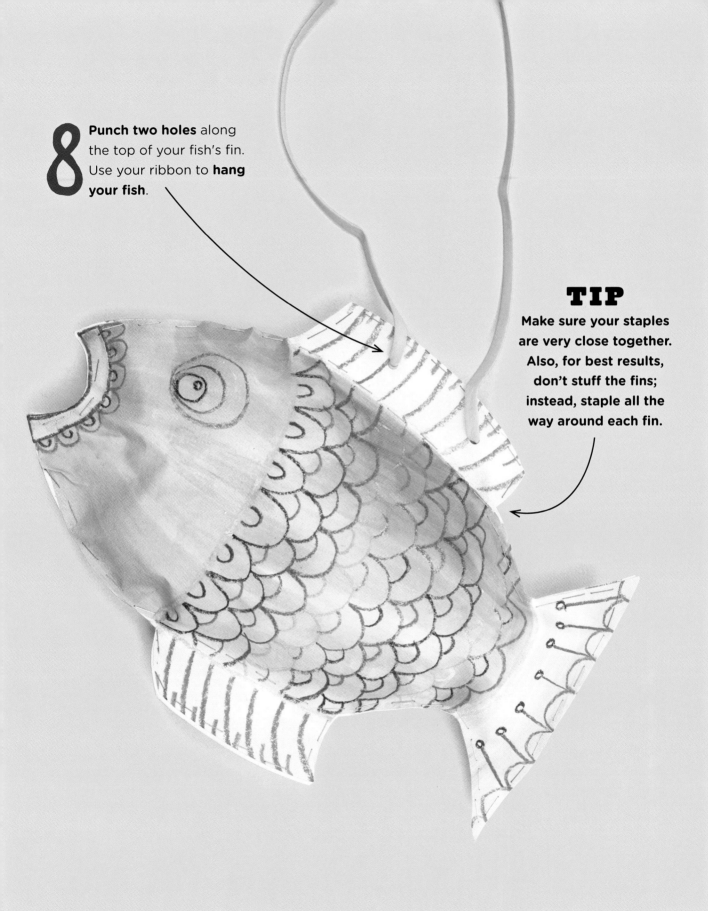

8 **Punch two holes** along the top of your fish's fin. Use your ribbon to **hang your fish**.

TIP
Make sure your staples are very close together. Also, for best results, don't stuff the fins; instead, staple all the way around each fin.

PAPIER-MÂCHÉ ALPACA

✂ ✂ ✂

+ a grown-up

WHAT YOU'LL NEED

- Newspaper
- Masking tape
- Large Styrofoam egg, 4 inches wide, or about the size of a softball
- 4 large nails (about 3 inches long)
- Colored tissue paper, torn into strips
- Mod Podge (or a half-and-half mix of white glue and water)
- Paintbrush
- Scissors
- Felt scraps
- Toothpicks
- Tacky glue
- 2 googly eyes
- Yarn and pom-poms (optional)

Alpacas are a very important part of Inca culture in Peru's Andes Mountains. Their soft, warm hair is used for clothing and blankets. Every year, Peruvians honor alpacas in a blessing ceremony, when they decorate the animals with flower petals, colorful pom-poms, and tassels.

Papier-mâché ("PAY-pur muh-SHAY") is a way of sculpting with wet materials that harden as they dry. We like using tissue paper and Mod Podge.

156

BUILDING THE BODY

1 **To make the neck, tightly roll the newspaper into a tube** about as long as a pencil and as thick as a Tootsie Roll. Secure the tube with tape, then tape the neck to the front of the Styrofoam egg, which will be your alpaca's body.

Your alpaca can be looking up, down, or sideways.

Fold newspaper into small triangles to make the ears.

2 Fold over about 1 inch of the newspaper tube to **make the head. Secure it with tape**. Then make the ears and tape them to the back of the head.

TIP
About 1 inch of the neck should be taped flat against the body. Otherwise the neck will be too wobbly.

3 Roll up a small bit of newspaper and tape it on the back end to **make a tail**.

4 With help from a grown-up, **make the legs** by sticking the nails into the bottom of the foam egg.

TAKE A STAND

After adding the head, neck, and tail, you may need to move the nail-legs around until your alpaca can stand up. If you do move any of the nails, wrap a little tape around where they go into the egg to make sure they stay in place.

When you tape on the ears you'll lose a little length, so try shaping them longer than you want your final ears.

continues on next page

PAPIER-MÂCHÉ YOUR ALPACA

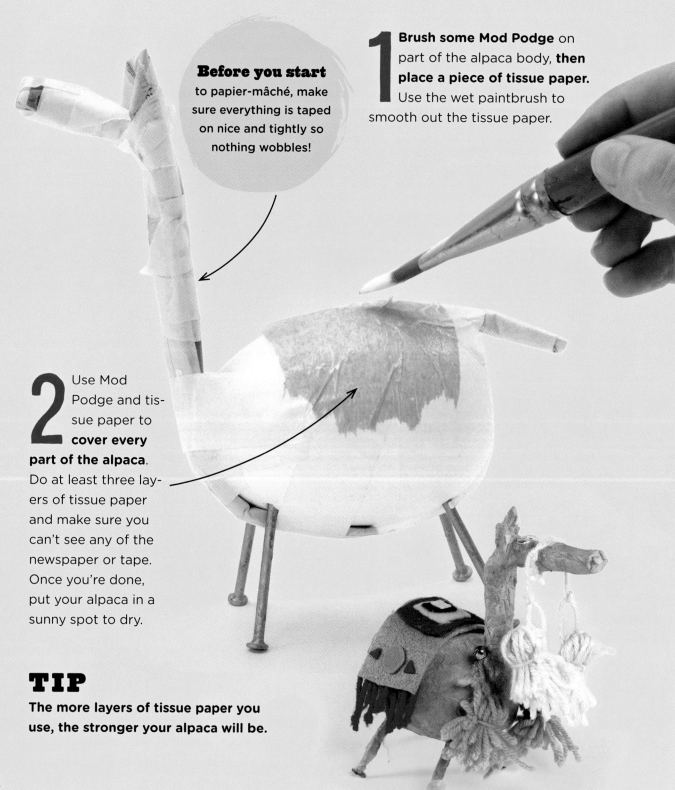

Before you start to papier-mâché, make sure everything is taped on nice and tightly so nothing wobbles!

1 Brush some Mod Podge on part of the alpaca body, **then place a piece of tissue paper.** Use the wet paintbrush to smooth out the tissue paper.

2 Use Mod Podge and tissue paper to **cover every part of the alpaca**. Do at least three layers of tissue paper and make sure you can't see any of the newspaper or tape. Once you're done, put your alpaca in a sunny spot to dry.

TIP
The more layers of tissue paper you use, the stronger your alpaca will be.

DECORATE YOUR ALPACA

1 While your alpaca is drying, **make its blanket**. Cut out a rectangle of felt to drape over the alpaca's back, then cut out other felt shapes to decorate the blanket. Attach the decorations using a toothpick and a little bit of tacky glue.

2 Once your alpaca is completely dry, use a toothpick and a tiny dab of tacky glue to **attach the googly eyes**.

TRY THIS

Use yarn to make little tassels or fringe for the blanket or to craft a tiny halter for your alpaca. Decorate its ears, feet, and tail with pom-poms. The more elaborate and colorful your alpaca, the happier it will be!

GiANT *PAPiER-MÂCHÉ ANiMAL

This is the largest project in the book, but it's lots of fun and you will amaze yourself with the result! We chose a fox for this example, but once you have the basics down, you can make whatever animal you want.

Tips *before* you begin:

You will use a lot of masking tape, so rip up at least eight 6-inch strips and stick them along the edge of the table. This way they will be ready when you need them.

Whenever you tape something, tape it up and down *and* back and forth. Taping in both directions will make it stronger.

Just as you would mold a ball of clay, mold the newspaper into the shape you want. Once you have a shape you like, use masking tape to make it stay.

1 **Stuff the paper bag** with scrunched-up newspaper until it's really full, and then tape closed the open end.

TIP

This is going to be the body of your animal, so not enough paper in the bag will make your animal's body too weak. You want the filled bag to be firm enough that you could toss it around like a ball.

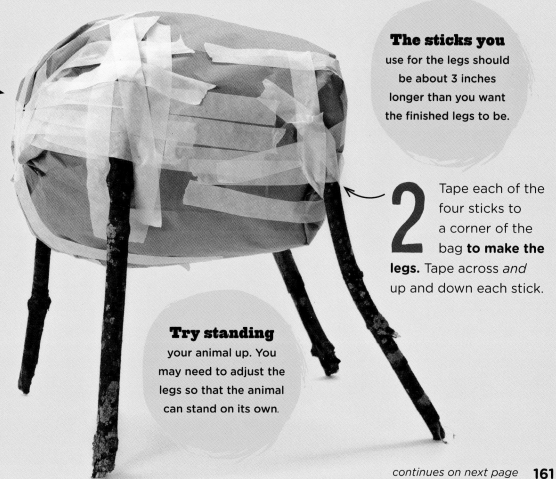

The sticks you use for the legs should be about 3 inches longer than you want the finished legs to be.

2 Tape each of the four sticks to a corner of the bag **to make the legs.** Tape across *and* up and down each stick.

Try standing your animal up. You may need to adjust the legs so that the animal can stand on its own.

continues on next page

3 Roll a tight ball of news-paper, then add more and more newspaper (like making a snowball!) **until the head is the size you want.** Mold this into the shape of the head. Tape it up really well.

4 **Make ears** by folding over a few sheets of newspaper the long way, then folding that in half the short way. Do this until the ears are the size and shape you want. Tape them to keep that shape. Then attach the ears to the back of the head.

5 Roll up full sheets of newspaper as thick as you want to **make the neck**. This tube should be about 6 inches longer than you want the finished neck to be, so that you have plenty of neck to attach to the body.

6 **Want to add a snout?** Mold another ball of newspaper into the shape you want, then tape it onto the head.

7 **Tape the head onto the neck.** Then lay the bottom of the neck against the body and attach it securely to the body.

TRY THIS

If your animal tips over, figure out where the problem is. Maybe one leg is too short or the head is too heavy. You can fix most problems with rocks: fill a piece of newspaper with a few rocks, scrunch up the paper, and tape it to the bottom of the short leg. If your animal tips forward, tape two bunches of rocks to its back feet. Then papier-mâché over your newspaper-and-rock additions.

Before you start to papier-mâché your animal, make sure nothing is loose or wobbly. Don't be afraid to use as much tape as you need to!

8 Brush **some Mod Podge** on part of the animal body, **then place a piece of tissue paper.** Use the paintbrush to smooth out the tissue paper.

9 Use Mod Podge and tissue paper to **cover every part of the animal**, adding as many layers as you need to cover the newspaper and tape. The more layers of tissue paper, the stronger your animal will be. After covering your animal, add eyes! Either scrunch up tissue paper into small balls and use Mod Podge to secure them to the head or glue on some buttons.

Let your animal dry in a sunny spot. This may take a few days.

MAKE IT YOURS

Once everything is attached to the body — but before you start to papier-mâché — add any details you'd like. Maybe your animal needs thicker legs, a tail, or a hunched back.

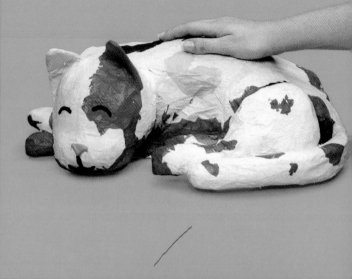

FUN

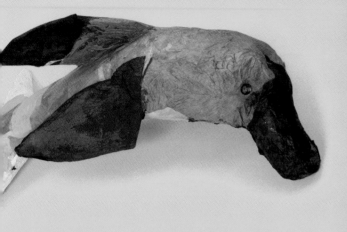

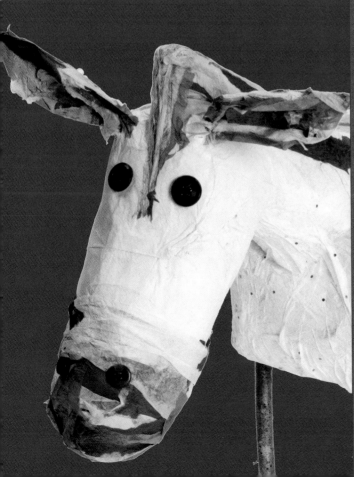

MEXiCAN CLAY SKULL

Edible treats known as sugar skulls, or *calaveras,* have been used in Mexican Day of the Dead celebrations for hundreds of years. This nonedible version is made of clay.

Traditional sugar skulls are very colorful, with lots of decorations.

1 **Roll the clay** into a ball about the size of a baseball.

2 Gently squeeze the sides of the ball to **make cheek bones**. Press your thumbs into the ball to **make eye sockets**.

Your skull is starting to take shape!

3 **Carve out details** using the toothpick: an upside-down V for the nostrils and lines to make the teeth.

4 **Decorate your skull** by pressing beads and/or sequins into the clay. Set it aside to dry.

5 Once the clay is dry, **color** or paint the eye sockets black. Then use other colors to **make your skull festive**.

TIP

Make the eyes sparkle! Add a small amount of glue inside the eye sockets and then sprinkle in some glitter.

ACKNOWLEDGMENTS

I want to thank my talented daughter, Olivia Tamzarian, who inspired me to create the Summer Art program; my husband, Rob Wilson, for his love, support, and encouragement throughout the book-writing process; my dear friends Daphne, Deb, Sheila, Marie, and The Goddesses, who have been there for me over the years; and Linda, who was there at the beginning. I want to extend an additional thank-you to Deanna Cook and Andrew Greto, who worked hard on this book and are also former Summer Art Barn parents and champions of the work we do. I especially want to thank my very good friend and coauthor Hilary for her awesome talent, technical expertise, and unlimited creativity.

— Marion Abrams

An enormous thank-you to my incredible parents, Marion and Chester Lay, who taught me the importance of kindness and creativity; to my sister, Gillian, for being my best friend and biggest cheerleader; to Karen Latuchie, good friend and author, for her writerly wisdom and guidance; to the late Bob Hugo, a titan of indie bookstores and my much-missed mentor, who would have loved to see this book in print; and to my husband, Isaac Jude Snell, for his enthusiastic daily affirmations of support while we wrote this book. And to my dear friend and coauthor Marion for creating this magical world of children's art and giving me the honor of being a part of it.

— HILARY EMERSON LAY

We both owe huge thank-yous to the following people from Storey Publishing: Deanna Cook, acquisitions editor, whose idea it was to write this book; Michal Lumsden, editor extraordinaire, who poured her dedication and humor into every project; Michaela Jebb, book designer, who spent so much time bringing this book to life; Sarah Chapman, copy editor, for her keen eye; Melinda Slaving, Jennifer Travis, and Alethea Morrison for handling all of the various forms, contracts, and permissions that went into this project; Hartley Batchelder for his Photoshop magic; Alee Moncy for publicizing our book so creatively; and the entire Storey and Workman sales teams (especially Maureen Karb) for their tireless efforts.

In addition, we'd like to thank Andrew Greto for his wonderful photographs; Randy Lotowycz and Angela Campbell of Workman Publishing for their answers and advice; Rob Wilson for so many things, including making us lunch every day while we wrote this book; and our 2018 guest teachers Eliza LaCroix, Katherine Anderson, Catherine Richotte, and Audrey Weston for helping us teach all 53 projects in this book over the course of one summer. And of course a huge thank-you to the thousands of kids, parents, and teachers who have brought their enthusiasm and imaginations to Summer Art Barn for 30 years.

A special thanks to all of the kids who participated in our 2018 camp and made the projects in this book:

Rose Abel-Zucker
Susannah Abel-Zucker
Ruby Aiken
Quinn Allen-Brezsnyak
Adelaide Amias
Taylor Barry
Teagan Barry
Maddy Battisti
Josephine Becker
Marissa Belina
Maya Berman-Lagier
Nils Berman-Lagier
Nora Biancardi
Noah Bradbury
Allyson Brittain
Nate Brody
Mary Burt
Sophie Calkins
Liza Cameron
Grace Caouette
Ava Carter-Meo
Katie Champoux
Nina Charland-Tait
Tali Cohen-Hamer
Chloe Comerford Hennessey
Ruby Corriveau-Roche
June Dalhaus
Lan Detenber
Emerson Dewitt
Finn Dewitt
Talya Eiseman
Adam Engel
Zoe Engel
Autumn Entin-O'Neil
Lucia Flajnik-Palladino
Gus Frey
Alana Fuqua
Lorenzo Gatrall

Mina Gatrall
Abigail Goff
Celia Goldsmith
Emma Gollis-Pedelaborde
Matthew Graham-Moga
Arlo Green
Lily Green
Lucy Grossman
Alice Hall
Jane Harrison-Millman
Miren Harrison-Millman
Kaleb Hayhurst
Reese Heston
Eisa Hiam
Piper Higuera
Penelope Hobbs
Evie Hodgeman
Gabriel Hodos-Rich
Sophie Hudzik
Avery Jackson
Jonah Jackson
Helen Jayne
Keene Jeffress
Rowan Jeffress
Gus Jenkins
Andrew Jones-Monahan
Rozlyn Kaufman
Benjamin Killip-Leonard
Zoe King
Cali Knox
Ana Kumar
Lucy Lackman
Eliza LaCroix
Nicholas Leigh
Rosie Mahoney
Emmy Maloney

Avery Mayer
Kate McCollough
John McVey
Lucy McVey
Reid McVey
Isabelle Micallef
Henry Michel
Sophie Michel
Anna Mignano
Lyla Miner
Harper Modestow
Ava Morris
Julia Morse
Tatum Morse
Thomas Neal
William Northrup
Sofia Oblomkova
Molly O'Brien
Maeve O'Neil
Helena Pagiar
Simone Pagiar
Bailey Park
Savvy Park
Alysha Parshall-Matylas
Jaxie Parshall-Matylas
Jyotica Partan
Rhys Potter-Hewes
Audrey Preer
Leah Reid
Isabella Reiter
Linnea Rhodes
Ezra Rich
Rylie Richards
Samuel Robbins
Zach Roberge
Owen Roch
Clara Rondina
Alex Rosen

Molly Rowlett
Lea Rubin-Esposito
Piper Russell Jones
Winnie Russell Jones
Quinn Sacco
Rowan Sakrejda-Leavitt
Stella Sakrejda-Leavitt
Hazel Sanderson
August Santos
Kaya Sarouhan
Coleman Schatz
Emmett Schatz
Nika Schenker
Laz Scher
Clara Schumann-Hobbs
Eliza Segal
Mattea Segal
Mira Serlin
Noli Sharp
Hadley Smith
Izzy Smith
Sydney Smith
Ronan Soergel
Alina Sorkin-Camacho
Isabel Sorkin-Camacho
Bea Tauer
Rosie Tauer
Eden Teperman
Nathan Thompson
Steven Thompson
Phoebe Todhunter
Julia Walkowicz
Elsie Woodruff
Jillian Worden
Elliott Wyman
Iris Young
Olivia Zaiken

If this is a library book, please photocopy these templates — don't cut them out of the book!

Stuffed Fish
Piece A
(page 152)
Join to piece B
Glue tab
Glue tab

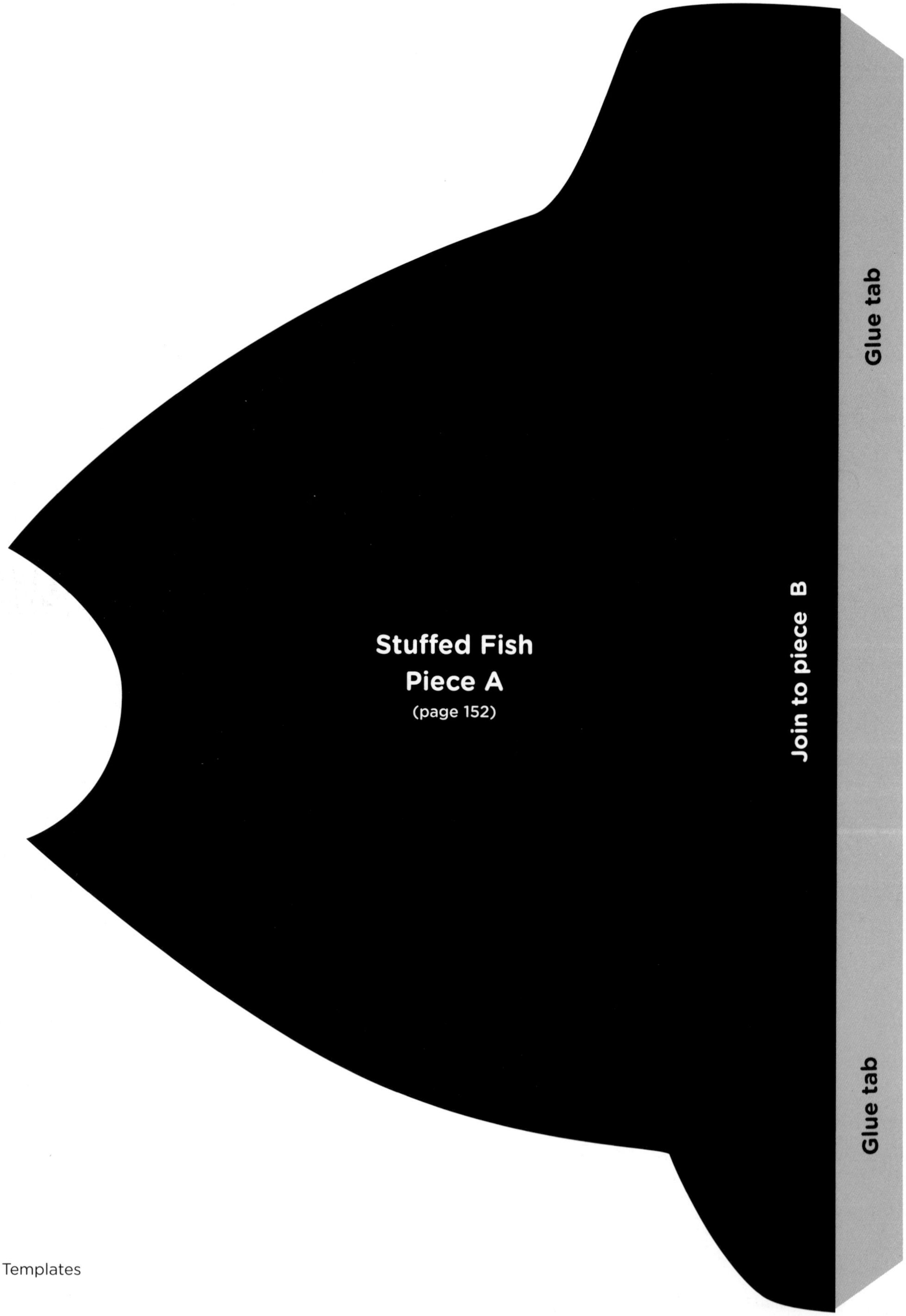

Join to piece A

Stuffed Fish
Piece B
(page 152)

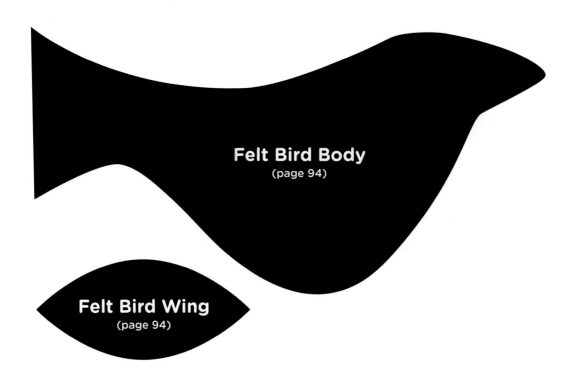

Felt Bird Body
(page 94)

Felt Bird Wing
(page 94)

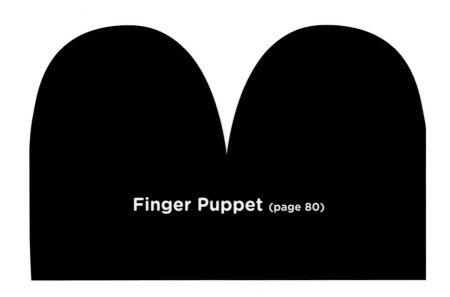

Finger Puppet (page 80)

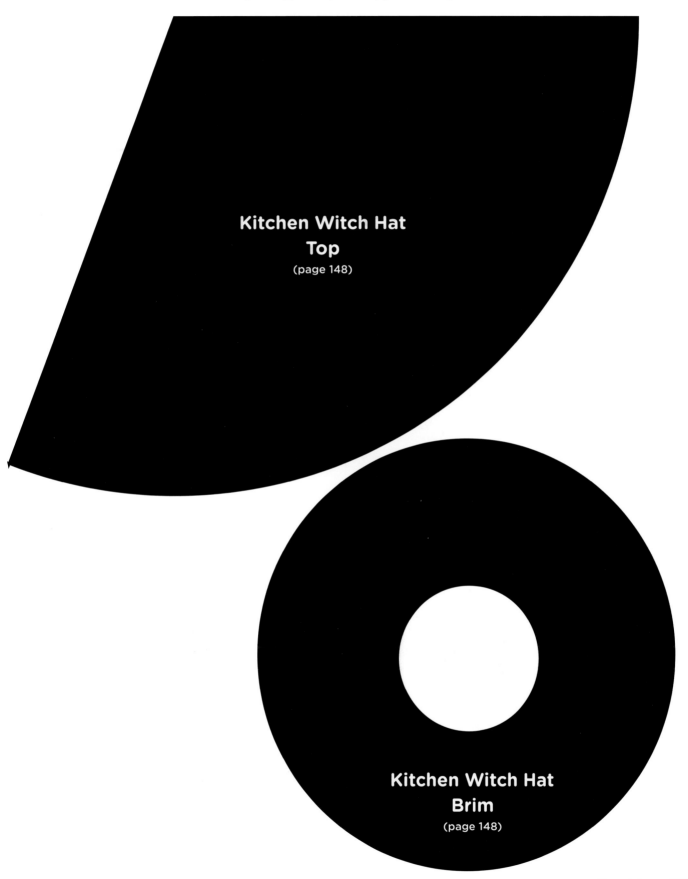

**Kitchen Witch Hat
Top**
(page 148)

**Kitchen Witch Hat
Brim**
(page 148)

If this is a library book, please photocopy these templates — don't cut them out of the book!

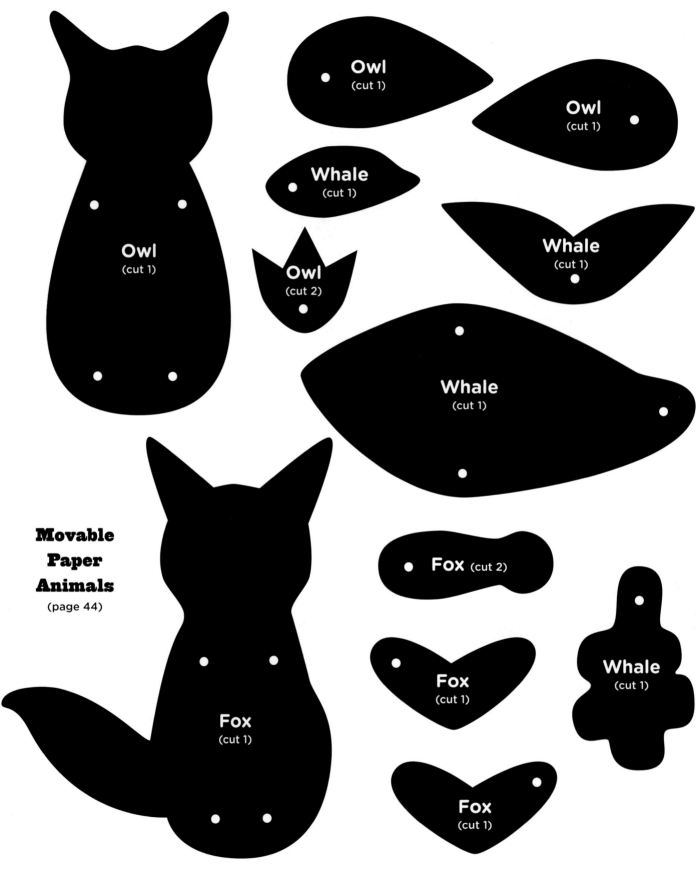

Owl (cut 1)

Owl (cut 1)

Whale (cut 1)

Owl (cut 1)

Whale (cut 1)

Owl (cut 2)

Whale (cut 1)

Movable Paper Animals

(page 44)

Fox (cut 2)

Fox (cut 1)

Whale (cut 1)

Fox (cut 1)

Fox (cut 1)

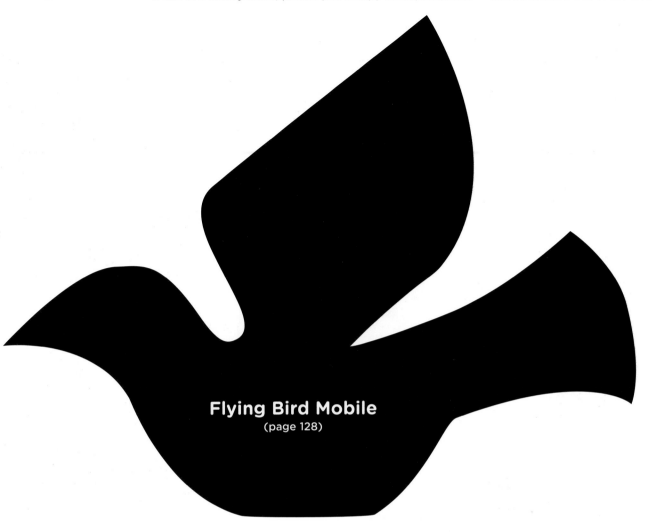

Flying Bird Mobile
(page 128)

Paper Bead
(page 60)

KeeP YOUR CReATiViTY FLOWing

with More Books from Storey

by Emily K. Neuburger
Make a visual day-in-your-life map, turn random splotches into quirky characters for a playful story, and list the things that make you *you*! These 60 interactive writing prompts and art how-tos will help spur your imaginative self-expression.

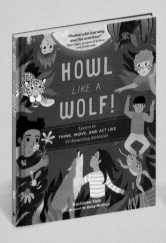

by Kathleen Yale
Balance an egg like an emperor penguin! Stalk like a camouflaged leopard! This lively illustrated guide to the animal kingdom introduces you to 15 birds, mammals, reptiles, and insects by explaining how to mimic each animal's movements, sounds, and behaviors.

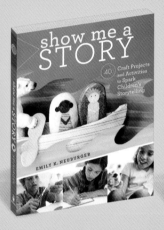

by Emily K. Neuburger
These 40 projects rev up your imagination. With the help of an original magnetic story board, memory cards, and word tags, you'll be brimming with fantastic tales before anyone can even say, "Once upon a time."

by Nicole Blum & Catherine Newman
Create, hack, or customize! Step-by-step directions show you the basics of how to sew, embroider, knit, crochet, weave, and felt. You can then use your new skills to hand-make cool bracelets, backpacks, merit badges, keychains, and more.